Journal of Biblical Literature
Monograph Series, Volume IV

THE DATE AND COMPOSITION
OF EZEKIEL

by

Carl Gordon Howie, Ph.D.

Society of Biblical Literature
222 North Fifteenth Street
Philadelphia 2, Pennsylvania
1950

THE DATE AND COMPOSITION
OF EZEKIEL

Copyright © 1960 by the Society of Biblical Literature
ISBN 1-58983-228-0

All rights reserved. No part of this work may be reproduced or transmitted in any form or by any means, electronic or mechanical, including photocopying and recording, or by means of any information storage or retrieval system, except as may be expressly permitted in writing from the publisher. Requests for permission should be addressed in writing to the Rights and Permissions Office, Society of Biblical Literature, 825 Houston Mill Road, Atlanta, GA 30329.

Printed in the United States of America
on acid-free paper

ABBREVIATIONS

AJSL	The American Journal of Semitic Languages and Literatures.
BASOR	The Bulletin of the American Schools of Oriental Research.
HTR	The Harvard Theological Review.
ICC	The International Critical Commentary.
JAOS	The Journal of the American Oriental Society.
JBL	The Journal of Biblical Literature.
JNES	The Journal of Near Eastern Studies.
JQR	The Jewish Quarterly Review.
LXX	Septuagint.
MT	Masoretic Text.
ZAW	Zeitschrift für die Alttestamentliche Wissenschaft.

Dr. Howie's monograph was originally submitted to the faculty of The Johns Hopkins University as a doctoral dissertation completed under the direction of Professor William F. Albright. While it is not the purpose of this Monograph Series to publish chiefly dissertations, the members of the Editoral Committee of the Society of Biblical Literature agree with the Editors of the Journal that dissertations of unusual merit have a place in this Series. The editorial consultants who read Dr. Howie's manuscript feel that he has contributed material of scholarly value in his treatment of archaeological and linguistic problems in the book of Ezekiel.

          Ralph Marcus
          Editor of the Monograph Series

PREFACE

THIS INTRODUCTORY STUDY of Ezekiel's prophecy grew from an interest in the book which dates back to theological seminary days. However, it was not until the writer began graduate work in Oriental Seminary, The Johns Hopkins University that he undertook serious research on the various critical problems of the book. He felt that recent archeological and linguistic material made a new study of the prophecy imperative.

The author is very grateful to Professor W.F. Albright for his invaluable guidance and help in the completion of this undertaking. Many of the ideas which are developed in the monograph originated with him; he edited the manuscript carefully and gave vital assistance in many other ways. Therefore, this volume is respectfully dedicated to WILLIAM FOXWELL ALBRIGHT, teacher and friend.

A special note of thanks goes to Dr. Frank Blake of The Johns Hopkins University, who gave generously of his time in correcting and editing Chapter III. Expressions of gratitude are also due Dr. John Bright, Dr. Harry Orlinsky and Dr. Ernest Wright for their help in the task of proof reading. Many of the suggestions of these three scholars have been incorporated in the final manuscript. In addition to these, the graciousness of Dr. Ralph Marcus in arranging for publication has been greatly appreciated. Except for his interest the manuscript would probably never have appeared in print.

Finally, the writer's wife has willingly given her time to the important but onerous job of typing. Her untiring help and inspiration have been important factors in the completion of this monograph.

Carl Gordon Howie
Lynchburg, Virginia

CONTENTS

	Page
Introduction	1
Chapters	
I. The Residence of Ezekiel	5
II. The Date of the Prophecy	27
III. The Aramaic in the Book of Ezekiel	47
IV. Psychological Aspects of Ezekiel and His Prophecy	69
V. The Composition of the Prophecy of Ezekiel	85
Conclusion	100
Footnotes	103

INTRODUCTION

THE PROPHECY of Ezekiel, written in apocalyptic style and replete with obscurities in text and meaning, has baffled more scholars and given rise to more strange ideas than perhaps any other book of the Bible. When the Jewish Canon was in process of formation, the authorities at first decided to reject Ezekiel, not because its inspiration was called in question, but rather because these leaders thought it wise to withdraw such a prophecy from public use lest the learned and half-learned be caused to stumble by the apparent discrepancies between it and the legal sections of the Pentateuch. Except for the insistance of Hananiah ben Hezekiah, the book which bears the name Ezekiel would probably have been omitted from the Jewish Canon. However, at the eleventh hour Hananiah by using 300 jars of oil as a means of "enlightenment" was able to produce a "profounder exegesis" for the passages which seemed to be out of keeping with the Tôrāh. In spite of this remarkable exegetical feat, which resulted in canonization for the work, the rabbis have been ever since trying to reconcile the legal differences between Ezekiel on the one hand and the Pentateuch on the other. Even in admitting this book to their canon, the Jews laid down definite reservations. The first chapter was made forbidden material for those under thirty and was never to be read at regular synagogue services lest it give rise to theosophical speculations.[1]

For centuries the prophecy was accepted by the Christian Church as extremely enigmatic but nonetheless profitable. Jerome despaired of ever understanding this profound work and likened the study of it to walking through catacombs where light seldom breaks through.[2] Calvin never finished his commentary on the book, and Luther put forth no major effort toward its interpretation.[3] Through all the years the prophecy has provided an excellent spawning place for millennialists of every sort. The Gog and Magog chapters (38-39) have been especially prolific in this respect.[4]

Among Jews and Christians Ezekiel was from earliest times accepted as the work of a true prophet who lived among the Babylonian gôlāh of 598 B.C. Never once from the time of canonization until the eighteenth century A.D. was this traditional position seriously challenged by a reputable scholar.

Minor divergences from this traditional opinion began with the appearance in 1771 of G.L. Oeder's Freye Untersuchung über einige Bücher des Alten Testaments, published posthumously by a friend at Halle. Oeder maintained in his book that 40-48 is a spurious addition to the prophecy.5 Soon afterward Heinrich Corrodi rejected Ez. 38-39 as well as 40-48.6 In 1832 Zunz brought out a monumental work, Die gottesdienstlichen Vorträge der Juden, in which he dated all the oracles of Ezekiel in the Persian period, not during the Babylonian captivity. Later he placed them more precisely between 440 and 400 B.C.7 L. Seinecke in his Geschichte des Volkes Israel, which appeared in 1876, proposed the theory that the prophecy is a pseudepigraphon written in 163 B.C. That date, he says, is clearly revealed in chapter 4. By subtracting 430 years from 593 B.C. one is able to arrive at what Seinecke considered the correct date. He equated Gog with Antiochus Epiphanes by a strange bit of letter-play (i.e., ANTIOCHUS = TIOCH = GOG).8 These and other conflicting views about our prophet received little attention and less support so that the book was left all but undisturbed by the rising tide of higher criticism. Even until quite recently this point of view held the field as illustrated by the following words written in 1933: "Corrupt as the text is in many places in Ezekiel, we have the rare satisfaction of studying a carefully elaborated prophecy whose authenticity is practically indisputed and indisputable."9 This statement reveals McFadyen either was unaware that the battle had already been joined on Ezekiel or simply refused to admit it.10 On the other hand, S.R. Driver was more accurate when in 1913 he wrote concerning Ezekiel: "No critical question arises in connection with the authorship of this book, the whole from beginning to end bearing unmistakably the mark of a single mind."11

Even though Kraetzschmar's and Herrmann's related works appeared in 1900 and 1908 respectively, neither represented an important deviation from the traditional view for both attributed most of the text to the prophet, proposing that two recensions of the book explained many of its difficulties.12 It was left for Gustav Hölscher to begin a new and radical attack on the text in 1925.13 Since that time the prophecy has received much attention from many scholars, but all efforts have resulted in no one acceptable conclusion about Ezekiel. The problem of this book has indeed become the problem of Old Testament studies since this prophecy was the pole-star on which much of our present dating of other books depends. A dislodgment of the traditional date would bring utter confusion of Biblical literary chronology as far as many scholars are concerned.14

There have been so far the three following major positions on Ezekiel criticism: (a)the book exhibits real unity and is

INTRODUCTION 3

the work of one mind, (b) the seeming unity is a later superimposed structure binding together independent pieces, (c) there is no unity at all. The last point of view has gained many adherents in recent years, but there are still other major difficulties in the book.

There is at present an amazing confusion and complete lack of agreement in works on the prophecy. The scholar who undertakes a study of the book is faced with literary problems which are legion. Not only is the prophecy written in apocalyptic style, its text is in very bad condition. As if such difficulties were not enough, we are confronted with a work whose authenticity is questioned in part or in its entirety, whose date is uncertain and whose traditional author is said by some to be the figment of a late Jewish imagination. Among those who agree that there is a kernel of genuine Ezekielian material in the prophecy there is no agreement as to where the book was written or to whom it was originally addressed. Was its locale Jerusalem, Jerusalem and Babylon, or Northern Israel and Mesopotamia? All three answers have been given with equal assurance and with what seems at first blush equal evidence. Literarily the book has the mark of one mind, and yet it is disconnected and disjointed in such a way as to preclude the possibility of its being the work of one hand or the product of one mind. So we face problems the difficulty of which can hardly be overestimated.

Our problem in this dissertation is to seek first an answer to the perplexing question concerning Ezekiel's residence. Was he, as tradition maintains, a prophet of the Babylonian gôlāh? If so, why does he speak as though in Judah and Jerusalem? Again if he resides among the captives of Babylon, why are his oracles directed toward Jerusalem? The Babylonian locale has been seriously called in question by many reputable scholars, and currently a majority seems to support a Palestinian locale for our prophet. It is our plan to examine the basis for this opinion and to see how well it stands up under criticism. Closely connected with the question of residence is the fixing of a date for the individual oracles. When did the prophet live? Is tradition accurate in dating the prophet or must the date be shifted? As a matter of fact, a major question is now simply: did Ezekiel live? The language of the book, which has generally been considered late since it contains Aramaic, has an important bearing on date. Linguistic data are of such value in solving our problem that detailed consideration of the Aramaic of Ezekiel and its bearing on the date has been undertaken.

Much controversy has revolved around the strange and complicated personality of Ezekiel, who has been psychoanalyzed more often than any other individual of the Old Testament. On account of the fact that certain psychological aspects of this man are directly pertinent to the question of residence, it is in order to discuss some of the attempts at psychoanalysis and to present side lights on the prophet's personality.

Finally the composition of the book itself presents the greatest difficulty. Many solutions have been offered as to how the prophecy assumed its present form. Irwin, Torrey, Herrmann, and a multitude of others have tried their hand, but we believe all were somewhat handicapped by their presuppositions. After a close examination of the text a detailed reconstruction of the literary evolution of the book will be sketched.

Our basic problem is to determine in so far as possible when and where Ezekiel lived. After that we hope to discover in general the manner by which this prophecy came into its present form.

Chapter I

THE RESIDENCE OF EZEKIEL

FOR CENTURIES information about a man Ezekiel contained in the book bearing that name was accepted at face value. It never occurred either to Jewish or Christian scholars to question the biographical or geographical background of the book. Ezekiel was a priest (Ez. 1:3) who in 598 B.C. was taken captive when Nebuchadrezzar carried the leaders of the Jewish community of Jerusalem into exile (II Kgs. 24:14). In the fifth year of Jehoiachin's captivity, 593 B.C. (Ez. 1:2), this exiled priest received a call to become the prophet of Yahweh among the captives at Tel-Abib on the River Chebar. The entire prophetic ministry of Ezekiel was spent in exile, and he never had the opportunity to return to Jerusalem in the flesh. However, he came often to the Holy City in spirit and frequently issued warnings of dire disaster against "the bloody city." After the destruction of Jerusalem the prophet turned his attention to the gôlāh. Instead of threats of violence and destruction his oracles were of a future restoration when God would rebuild the waste places (Ez. 35-36) and revive the nation (Ez. 37).

Conditions under which the prophet and other members of the gôlāh were forced to live could have been much worse. The prophet had a house (20:1) and was married (24:18). There was probably sufficient food since we hear of no distress and since the description of famine in chapters 4 and 5 is most probably visionary, as we shall attempt to show below.

According to tradition, Ezekiel lived among the gôlāh, but he had a strange ability to be transported in spirit to familiar scenes either of childhood or later life. His personality was extremely complex, partaking as it did both of prophetic fire and pedantic priestly care for ceremonial technicalities and exactitude. He was a man in whom many forces were joined, and hence he cannot be judged according to normal standards.

The great contribution of Ezekiel to the future of Judaism was made in his visions of the restored Temple and land (Ez. 40-48). The magnificent plan for the future which appeared to the prophet on the fourteenth anniversary of the city's fall was most probably a rallying point for resurgent Judaism a half century later. Many still consider Ezekiel to be the man who laid the foundations of Judaism even though Ezra was the real builder.

In summary, therefore, tradition, which held the field for over 2000 years, puts Ezekiel in Babylon, where he lived out his ministry and life. Only in spirit did the great prophet of the captivity return to his beloved homeland. Essentially this same point of view is still supported by W.F. Albright, G.A. Cooke, Rudolph Kittel, Adolphe Lods, J.E. McFadyen, Otto Eissfeldt, Ernst Sellin, Joseph Ziegler and many other scholars, Catholic, Jewish and Protestant.[1]

For more than two decades, however, this traditional opinion has been under constant criticism. The nub of the difficulty rests on the improbability of a prophet's speaking to an audience which was not immediately at hand. Ezekiel seems to be in Jerusalem among rebellious people, and yet he claims to be in Babylon with the exiles. Usually a prophet carried out his calling in the midst of those for whom his oracles were meant. Ezekiel's passionate appeals and symbolic actions lead some to conclude that he was facing his audience.[2] It is because of this seemingly insurmountable difficulty that many scholars no longer accept the Babylonian locale and try to substitute for it a Palestinian residence.

Those who find themselves unable to accept a Babylonian residence for Ezekiel have been able to offer very plausible arguments against the traditional position. Major reasons may be summed up under eight headings. (1)The prophet's commission was to the House of Israel, as is plainly stated in several references.

"And he said unto me, Son of man, I send thee to the children of Israel. . ." (2:3)

"And he said unto me, Son of man, eat that which thou findest; eat this roll, and go, speak unto the house of Israel." (3:1)

"And he said unto me, Son of man, go get thee unto the house of Israel, and speak with my words unto them. For thou art not sent unto a people of a strange speech and of a hard language, but to the house of Israel." (3:4-5)

Only twice, according to critics of the Babylonian locale, does the term "House of Israel" clearly have reference to the Babylonian gôlāh (cf. 11:15; 37:16). Ezekiel was appointed by Yahweh to be a watchman over the Israelites and to warn them against their evil ways (3:16-21; 18:1-32; 33:1-20). These Israelites could be none other than the inhabitants of Jerusalem

THE RESIDENCE OF EZEKIEL 7

and Judah since one would hardly expect Ezekiel to speak in
such a way about the "good figs" of the Exile (cf. Jer. 24).
Against what could the prophet possibly be warning those who
were already in Exile? Reference is made to the coming destruction of Jerusalem in 9:4-5 and 14:12-20 with the condition
that only the penitent ones shall escape.

(2) The prophet, whose book locates him in Babylon, actually
addressed the people of Judah and Jerusalem so directly as to
give one the impression that speaker and audience are face to
face.
  "Son of man, cause Jerusalem to know her abominations."
(16:2)

  "Say unto them, Thus saith the Lord Yahweh: this burden
  concerneth the prince in Jerusalem and all the house
  of Israel among whom they are. Say, I am your sign:
  like as I have done so shall it be done unto them; they
  shall go into Exile, into captivity." (12:10-11)
Apparently in the last reference the prophet could not possibly
be talking to the captives at Tel-Abib since he predicts an
exile yet to be. Other instances where the prophet is commanded
to speak to the people in Palestine are found in 6:2, 7:2, 21:
7 and 22:2-3. An alternative possibility, namely, that the oracles could originally have been written, must be ruled out because Ezekiel is always commanded to speak, never to write.

(3) The prophecies which are found in the book as it now
stands would have been completely irrelevant for the exiles at
Tel-Abib. Were they the rebellious house whom the prophet was
commanded to warn against the coming destruction (Ez. 2-3; 22)?
Was it the unfortunate gôlāh which the prophet condemned for
idolatry on high places and more specifically for the worship
of Moloch (20:33)? Apparently Ezekiel was warning the rebellious house of Jerusalem and spoke of the multitudinous sins in
the condemnation of a visible audience. If indeed the Babylonian residence is correct, then the situation is a peculiar one.
An exiled prophet condemned by word and act a segment of his
dismembered nation which was miles beyond the sound of his
voice. All the while he had practically no direct message for
the people among whom he lived. Such a prophetic career as is
recorded in Ez. 1-24 could make sense only in a Palestinian locale in the years immediately preceding the Fall in Jerusalem
in 587 B.C.

(4) Several verbal references imply that Ezekiel was actually
in Jerusalem. For example, he is told to "look toward the south"
in 21:1 and later is commanded to do an about face toward the

Holy City (21:6). Such references definitely imply that the prophet was really on the scene at the time. The likelihood that the Jews had become a self-governing body in Babylon in such a short time is practically nil, hence the mention of the elders of Judah and Israel is another indication that Ezekiel spent at least the first part of his ministry in Jerusalem.

(5) The prophet's intimate, first hand knowledge of conditions in and about Jerusalem makes it necessary to assume that, in spite of statements to the contrary, he was a part of the life of the city. He was aware of the internal political intrigues in the tug-of-war between pro-Egyptian and pro-Babylonian factions in the capital (17:13-18; 23:19-21); he also knew of economic conditions inside the walls and the distress brought on by the siege (7:12-13), and most important he was cognizant of the general mood of the people (12:21-28). Possession of such detailed information would be incredible had Ezekiel been in Babylon.

(6) Acceptance of a Palestinian locale would eliminate the necessity for assuming the gift of second sight on Ezekiel's part. For generations devout exegetes have believed that Ezekiel had the power to see things as they happened in distant places, thus explaining his remarkable descriptions of Jerusalem life while he remained in Babylon. This amazing gift was a satisfactory solution to the residence question in by-gone days, but modern science has rendered it invalid. If, as opponents of the Babylonian locale believe, Ezekiel actually lived in Jerusalem, not in Babylon, and saw the sights he reported, then the difficulty which modern minds have in accepting clairvoyance is immediately solved.

(7) The symbolic actions of Ezekiel would be completely meaningless in Babylon but would be a dramatic and forceful warning in Palestine. Why would a prophet who lived in Babylon go through the motions of a man in flight from doomed Jerusalem when he was speaking to people who had already fled and were now living in exile (Ez. 12)? Strange shows such as those described in Ez. 4 and 5 would have absolutely no significance for a people in Babylon. Any prophecy which is acted out must have an immediate audience to attain real effectiveness. It stands to reason therefore that these symbolic actions must have had their setting in Palestine.

(8) Babylonian elements that have been pointed out in the prophecy can easily be explained on other grounds. By accepting the work of one or more Babylonian redactors the student is able to restore the original Palestinian locale of the pro-

phet's work. If one will remove the following topographical references, then the Babylonian residence is destroyed:

". . .as I was among the captives by the river Chebar. . ." (1:1b)

". . .in the land of the Chaldeans by the river Chebar. . ." (1:3b)

"And go, get thee to them of the captivity. . ." (3:11a)

"Then I came to them of the captivity at Tel-Abib that dwelt by the river Chebar, and to where they dwelt and I sat there overwhelmed among them seven days." (3:15)

". . .the glory of Yahweh stood there as the glory which I saw by the river Chebar. . ." (3:23)

". . .this is the living creature that I saw by the river Chebar." (10:15b)

"This is the living creature that I saw under the God of Israel by the river Chebar. . ." (10:20a)

"And as for the likeness of their faces which I saw by the river Chebar. . ." (10:22a)

"And the Spirit lifted me up and brought me in vision by the Spirit of God into Chaldea, to them of the captivity. . . .Then I spoke unto them of the captivity all the things that Yahweh had showed me." (11:24-25)

After the excision of these brief Babylonian topographical verses, the book takes on a complete Palestinian atmosphere.[3]

On these eight major areas of argument rests the case of those who would shift the residence of Ezekiel in part or completely from Babylon. Other minor reasons for challenging the traditional opinion are given from time to time, but generally speaking, the criticisms discussed above represent the foundation for questioning a Babylonian locale.[4] As we review individual treatments of the problem, other minor arguments will be pointed out.

Although there is general agreement among most scholars in their reasons for doubting a Babylonian residence, hardly any area of agreement exists in the resulting pictures of Ezekiel, the man and the book. There have been several major attempts at reconstruction of the geographical background of the prophecy, and these have received widespread support from scholars of varying schools of thought. Before any analysis of the general attack is made, an objective sketch of the variations from the traditional residential position should be presented.

Volkmar Herntrich maintains that Ezekiel's ministry had a Palestinian setting and that most of the oracles of Ez. 2-24 were addressed directly to the people of Jerusalem. The prophet actually went through the Temple and saw the religious syncretism as described in chapter 8. The expression, "Yahweh brought me," means that God moved the will of Ezekiel to make this trip through the holy precincts. With Ezekiel in Palestine the Pelatiah problem is completely solved. For a long time students of the book have wondered how a prophet's denunciation spoken in Babylon could possibly bring about the death of a man living in Jerusalem (cf. 11:13). Had the men been face to face such an occurrence would be clearly within the realm of probability. Herntrich concludes that all the genuine oracles which are contained in Ez. 1-39 were given by Ezekiel in Palestine before 587 B.C. Even though he is not absolutely certain as to the date of the prophet, Herntrich does not think he ever prophesied again after 587 B.C. The major argument of Herntrich against a residence among the gôlāh is the fact that the book gives no details about the exiled King Jehoiachin nor does it portray conditions under which the gôlāh lived. This reason plus these mentioned earlier in the chapter are adequate basis for discounting a Babylonian locale, according to Herntrich.

Herntrich sees in the prophecy as it now stands the reflection of two different worlds: the world of Ezekiel, who was a great prophet, and the world of a later redactor who gave the book its Babylonian setting and made Ezekiel a member of the captive band which was exiled to Babylon in 598 B.C. Not only did the redactor frame the book in a Babylonian setting, he added the strange visionary material of chapters 1, 9 and 10 along with the framework of Ez. 2, 3, 8 and 11. Other small pieces such as 14:21-23 and 33:30-33 are attributed to his hand. Finally the great contribution of the Redactor was made in Ez. 40-48 where he presents a religious program for the future. The date in 40:1 is no more than a piece of fiction which is part of the superimposed framework added either by a circle or individual in Babylon.

Ezekiel was, therefore, according to Herntrich, a prophet in the true sense of the word exercising his ministry in Jerusalem between 598 and 587 B.C. He never was in Babylon, and such a place as Tel-Abib is redactional fiction. The whole Babylonian framework of the book along with the visionary material is the work of a Babylonian redactor who was probably among the captive Jews of 598 B.C.[5]

I.G. Matthews agrees with Herntrich about the scene of Ez. 1-24, but from there on the opinions of these two scholars diverge considerably. Matthews feels that many of the oracles in chapters 1-24 were delivered in person under siege, actual or threatened, probably between 590-586 B.C.[6] He admits a second phase to the prophet's activity which lasted as late as 570 B.C. (29:17), but he is not sure about the setting for these late oracles. Whether Ezekiel ever went to Babylon, according to Matthews, must forever remain a question. Perhaps the prophet lived out his latter years in Phoenicia, North Israel or even Egypt. A case could be made for any of these places from indirect evidence contained in the prophecy. A Babylonian redactor added much of the visionary material as well as chapters 40-48 between 520 and 500 B.C.[7]

J.B. Harford locates the prophet in Palestine arguing that most of the time "house of Israel" is the name used for the population of Judah and Israel.[8]

Of major significance for the question of residence is the study of Ezekiel by A. Bertholet, which appeared in 1936. In his commentary he presented for the first time his three-residence theory of Ezekiel's prophetic activity. The initial call to prophecy came to Ezekiel at Jerusalem in 593 B.C. (2:3-3:9) when he was commissioned to speak to "a rebellious house." For the next six years he exercised his ministry of warning the people of Jerusalem and Judah as he had been commanded to do. Prior to the fall of the city, but during the siege, the prophet moved ostentatiously to a village in Judah (12:3), and it was there that news of the city's destruction in 587 B.C. was received (33:21). In other words, Bertholet sees in the incidents depicted in chapter 12, not just a symbolic action, but a real removal of the prophet from the doomed city. Thereafter he left for Babylon, where a second visionary call to prophecy was received (1:4-2:2) in the thirteenth year of Jehoiachin's captivity 585 B.C. By reading thirteenth for thirtieth in Ez. 1:1, Bertholet arrives at this date for the beginning of the Babylonian career of the prophet. Thus Bertholet in his book attributes most of the prophecy to Ezekiel whether spoken in Jerusalem or Babylon. He divides the material up between these two locales and thus solves to his own satisfaction the question of residence.[9]

In a recent article P. Auvray follows Bertholet's position practically word for word. He thinks that it was necessary for the prophet to leave Jerusalem and move to a nearby village in

Judah in order that he might avoid the terrible danger of a city under siege. After writing the oracles against the nations, about six months from the time of Jerusalem's destruction, Ezekiel went to Babylon, where he lived the remainder of his life. That in brief is Auvray's position.[10]

Basically the same judgment is given by Van den Born. He does not follow Bertholet and Auvray in the theory that Ezekiel moved temporarily to a village prior to the Fall of the Holy City, but he does hold that the prophet was in Palestine prior to 586 B.C. and in Babylon after that date.[11]

O.R. Fisher presents a different explanation of the residence issue. He contends that the prophet was deported with the exiles of 598 B.C. as the book plainly states and as tradition has maintained. In the fifth year of that captivity Ezekiel was called in a vision which occurred in Babylon to be a prophet to the people of Judah (2:3). Immediately the priest-prophet, in response to this divine calling, made his way back to Jerusalem. In the course of his prophetic ministry there he saw pagan rites in the Temple and other disturbing scenes described in Ez. 8. There among his fellow countrymen Ezekiel delivered his oracles of destruction against the inhabitants of the land (2:1-3:9; 4-7; 12-24). This man of God remained in the doomed city throughout the siege during which time his wife died. He was an eyewitness to the looting and capture of the city (Ez.9). In vision he saw Yahweh preparing to leave the Temple (Ez.10). After the destruction of Jerusalem had been accomplished, our prophet was given another commission: to return to the captive Jews of Babylon with a message of hope and encouragement (34-48). Ezekiel probably edited his own book, but it was later revised by redactors.[12] D.N. Freedman supports almost exactly this same judgment concerning the problem of residence in his unpublished thesis, *The Theology of Ezekiel*.[13]

Oesterley and Robinson have reached conclusions slightly different from any of those described above. According to their view, the ministry of Ezekiel began in 602 B.C.; and his prophecies of doom, uttered during the reign of Jehoiakim, were quickly put into writing. In 598 B.C. he was carried captive, took the prophecies with him and added the oracles of restoration in Babylon. Later editors worked the book over in order to give it a thorough Babylonian background.[14]

One of the most radical and at the same time most interesting commentaries on the work of Ezekiel is C.C. Torrey's *Pseudo-Ezekiel and the Original Prophecy*. Since a thorough-going exposition and criticism of this work logically comes under a discussion of date, we shall return to it in chapter II. Suffice it to say at this point that Torrey places the pseudo-prophet in Palestine and attributes the Babylonian setting to a later redactor.[15]

Soon after Pseudo-Ezekiel appeared, James Smith published The Book of the Prophet Ezekiel, in which he adopted a position similar to that of Torrey, even though neither man knew the other was working on the problem. Smith attempted to show that Ezekiel, a real historical figure, lived and prophesied in the time of Manasseh. He presents the following points in support of this unusual contention: (1) Neither Kings nor Jeremiah mention a prophet Ezekiel. (2) In the text it is clearly stated that our prophet went "among the exiles." (3) Nowhere in the prophecy do we find a description of the living conditions of the gôlāh. (4) Religious recognition of the national god was not required in the neo-Babylonian Empire, but in the late Assyrian Empire such a requirement was strictly enforced. (5) The time of Manasseh's reign fits perfectly the religious situation described by the prophet, e.g., sun worship, Baal and Astarte cults. (6) In the Talmud there is a significant passage which states that prior to this vision of Yahweh in Chaldea, Ezekiel exercised his prophetic office in Palestine. (7) Dates contained in the prophecy are mostly artificial, but even if they prove true, it does not necessarily follow that all material between two given dates belongs there chronologically.[16]

Smith believes that Ezekiel was a native of North Israel for several reasons: (1) "House of Israel" apparently is the name used for the Northern Kingdom and has absolutely no connection with Judah. (2) The idolatries described in chapter 6 are characteristic of the North. (3) Oracles against the false prophets contained in Ez. 13 are more applicable to Israel than to Judah. (4) The popular simile of the vine (Ez. 15) was used by North Country prophets. (5) Ezekiel in line with a Northern tradition traces the origin of Jerusalem to Amorite and Hittite parentage. (6) In chapter 23 the sin of Judah is more heinous than that of Israel. These points along with other alleged evidence lead Smith to conclude that Ezekiel was a native of the North, who prophesied during the reign of Manasseh. Part of the ministry of this Northern prophet was spent in Palestine, and the rest was lived out among the diaspora of North Israel. The two sections of prophetic oracles were later united by a redactor, who gave them a Babylonian setting.[17]

With Smith's work our survey of the important variations on the long standing traditional view of Ezekiel's residence is complete. In first sketching the major reasons for discounting the Babylonian locale it was our purpose to show clearly the reason scholars found it necessary to suggest alternatives. We have attempted to be objective and non-critical in relating arguments and positions of scholars who alter the traditional view of the book. Now, however, these arguments must be weighed, and all positions must be examined. Our method in this chapter will be to discuss each argument in order of its appearance above.

Much disagreement has revolved around the meaning of the term "house of Israel" and similar expressions in Ezekiel. To what did the prophet have reference? Some claim, with James Smith, that the abundant usage of Israel (183 times in the book) indicates a North Israelite background. Many who deny a Babylonian locale point to this terminology as strong evidence favoring Palestinian residence.[18] Fortunately for us, G.A. Danell has made a careful study of the occurrences of the name in Ezekiel's prophecy. Danell concludes that the name Israel as used by the prophet in chapters 1 to 24 has no uniform sense. It often is used as the exiled community (3:7; 4:3; 12:9; 18:25, 29, 30, 31 et al), but the people living in Jerusalem and Judah are also called by the name (4:13; 6:5, 11; 14:1, 7; 20:1). At least on two occasions the word definitely points to North Israel (4:4; 9:9). Finally, it sometimes encompasses the whole people (e.g., 4:3, 14:8, 9).[19] Danell's study definitely weakens the argument for a Palestinian locale based on the use of this term.

Proponents of a Palestinian setting point out that Ezekiel was called to be a watchman over Israel to warn them against their wickedness. Presumably, in the light of the above mentioned study, Israel in Ezekiel's mind meant both segments of the nation, those left behind in Judah and those already in Babylon. The prophet had a dual mission, namely, to point the lesson of history contained in Jerusalem's downfall and to preserve a spiritual remnant in captivity as the nucleus for a revived society.[20]

It has been considered quite strange that any prophet should be hundreds of miles removed from the people to whom his words were directed. What possible value could his threats of disaster and calls to repentance have on the people in Palestine while he was in Babylon? In order to solve this problem scholars have unhappily shifted the setting for these oracles to Judah and Jerusalem. It is an admitted fact that audiences which actually heard the prophecies of men like Amos, Micah, Jeremiah and others were small. Their messages were spread verbally by a chosen few who heard the oracles first hand. We maintain that Ezekiel used a similar technique in "sending" his messages back to the people of Jerusalem. He knew very well that his words were not evaporating into thin air but was convinced that eventually they would find their way to the people for whom he had originally intended them. That there was contact between Jerusalem and Tel-Abib is known from Jeremiah's letter to the exiles (Jer. 29).[21]

The foreign nations prophecies of Isaiah, Nahum, Zephaniah and Jeremiah give added support to the possibility of Ezekiel's speaking to an unseen audience. Certainly nobody claims that these prophets faced foreign audiences directly.[22] It is also true that oracles against kings were seldom delivered face to face (cf. Jer. 22). One wonders how often any prophet stood in the presence of those for whom his words were intended. At best he stood before a fraction of his intended audience.

Those who argue for the necessity of the prophet's facing his audience have overlooked the belief current in Ezekiel's time that the word of Yahweh once spoken would have its own effect. If therefore Yahweh commanded Ezekiel to prophesy in Babylon, the prophet would do so and consider his mission completed. He would not be concerned with his audience as speakers are today because the word once spoken in the name of Yahweh would make itself felt. There is no reason to doubt a Babylonian locale on account of the fallacious reasoning that a prophet must face his audience directly.

Central among the points of difficulty raised by the acceptance of the Babylonian setting is the question: were the oracles of Ezekiel irrelevant for the gôlāh? At least in chapters 1 to 24 the prophet is primarily concerned with predicting the utter destruction of Jerusalem. Already the people in Babylon had lived through a siege and the long trek to captivity in a strange land. Those who raise such issues forget that Israel's people might be temporarily separated, but there still was only one Israel in the minds of the exiles at Tel-Abib. The claim that no words were addressed directly to the gôlāh betrays a misunderstanding of the fact that these captives never felt themselves completely cut off from Israel, but felt rather that they were still a part of God's chosen even though forced to live for awhile in Babylon. These folk were therefore vitally concerned with the fate of their native land, to which one day they hoped to return.[23]

There is a very real relevance to Ezekiel's oracles against Jerusalem even for those already exiled. Jerusalem had become a symbol of impregnability in the minds of many Jews since the remarkable deliverance of the city from Sennacherib in 701 B.C. As long as the ancient city stood, there was hope for a quick return. Both Jeremiah (Jer. 29) and Ezekiel did their best to extinguish these fires of easy optimism. So the words against Judah prepared the exiles for their cruel but important destiny while serving as a warning to an unseen assemblage.

Scholars have expressed surprise that elders should be found at Tel-Abib so soon after the Jews had been brought to Babylon (8:1; 14:1; 20:1). On the contrary, it would be more surprising if there were not elders carried away from Jerusalem in 598B.C. since those left behind are described as "the poorest sort of the people of the land" (II Kgs. 24:14). Certainly the elders must have been among the official class that was deported by the Neo-Babylonian king. Further testimony that elders were among the Jews in Babylon is provided in Jeremiah's letter which was addressed to the "elders of the captivity" (Jer. 29:1). Whether there was much self government at Tel-Abib remains a question, but that there were elders on the scene is beyond question.[24]

On the other hand, it is possible that at least one or perhaps all the visits which the elders paid Ezekiel were real pilgrimages of officials from Jerusalem, but the probability is very unlikely for several reasons. The Babylonians would hardly allow such an official trip which might reunite the troublesome vassal state. We doubt that the elders would be especially anxious to seek the advice of one who was constantly predicting the undoing of their native city. Beyond reasonable doubt those elders referred to in Ezekiel were resident in Babylon.[25]

Serious consideration should not be given to the ridiculous contention that Ezekiel in order to "look toward the South" (20:46) or to set his face "toward Jerusalem" (21:1) would necessarily have to be physically on the scene. Indeed critics have gone too far in claiming that the prophet had such a poor memory as to forget familiar scenes after being away from them a few short years. This recollection of the general topography in and around Jerusalem is to be expected unless we take Ezekiel to be an unbelievably stupid person, whose memory was no longer than his field of vision.

Ezekiel's intimate, seemingly first hand, knowledge of conditions existing in Jerusalem has been used often to show that the prophet was in his native land. Such reasoning would carry more weight except for Jeremiah's letter to the gôlāh, reflecting as it does considerable information about conditions among

the captives (Jer. 29). It is reasonably certain that Ezekiel
knew at least as much about Jerusalem, whose environs and people were familiar to him, as Jeremiah did about the exiles of
Tel-Abib.

As for the political tug-of-war between pro-Egyptian and
pro-Babylonian forces, that had been going on since the battle
of Megiddo, when Judah became a vassal of Egypt. In 605 B.C.
following the battle of Carchemish, Babylon took over the country, but afterwards there was a strong tendency to look to
Egypt for deliverance. Indeed successful action on the part of
an Egyptian army against the Chaldeans would possibly have
meant a restoration for the gôlāh, so one can be sure that word
of this struggle as it developed made its way quickly to Tel-
Abib. It would be surprising if Ezekiel had not taken note of
this titanic contest on which the immediate fate of his fellow
captives depended (17:13-18; 23:19-21).[26]

In every discussion of this problem which we have read one
very important fact has been completely neglected. Our prophet
had lived through the siege which led to Jehoiachin's surrender
in 598 B.C. and so had a first hand knowledge of conditions
that prevail in a besieged city. Life in a besieged city when-
ever and wherever it may be is the same. It is not so incredible, therefore, that our prophet described, albeit in a general
way, the confusion and consternation which was the lot of the
besieged citizenry (7:12-13) as well as the extremes to which
hunger can drive men (5:10). One must admit the definite probability that the popular proverbs recorded in 12:21-28 had their
origin during the first siege prior to the captivity of 598
B.C. and regained usage during the second siege of 587 B.C.[27]

The argument that a Palestinian locale would eliminate the
necessity of clairvoyance is at best most unscientific. To deny
clairvoyance *a priori*, especially at a time when experiments
are being conducted, reveals a dogmatic approach which might
well block the way to a proper solution. Our discussion of this
problem is found in chapter IV, hence further attention at this
time is unnecessary.

A major point in the case of those who call in question a
Babylonian residence is the belief that the symbolic actions of
Ezekiel would have little or no meaning at Tel-Abib but would
be dramatic presentation of important themes if acted out in
Jerusalem. At first glance, this interpretation seems plausible, but on closer examination one realizes that it is based on
the unproven assumption that the prophet was in Palestine. In
other words, if the Palestinian locale were established on the

basis of other evidence, this point might have some validity. However if one assumes a Babylonian locale in line with tradition, it is not of value. Chapter 4 is best explained as a vision (cf. Chapter IV). As we have pointed out above, the fate of Judah and Jerusalem, whether predicted by word of mouth or in symbolic actions, would have definite relevance to the gōlāh. Certain objects used in these little dramas indicate clearly that they were enacted on a Babylonian setting.

In 4:1 the prophet is commanded to take a לְבֵנָה and draw on it the map of Jerusalem, which would be quite an unusual action in Judah, but such maps were common in the Neo-Babylonian Empire. This term לְבֵנָה regularly refers to sun-dried brick in the Bible and not to tile, as Torrey would have his readers think.29

More important is the fact that Ezekiel is commanded "to dig through" the walls of a house in his removal from the doomed city. The Hebrew word used is חתר. It has been pointed out by W.F. Albright, from experience with stone walls at Tell Beit Mirsim and other towns of Judah all over the hill country of Palestine in that general period, that such a hole dug through the ordinary stone walls of the preëxilic period in Palestine would have brought about immediate collapse of the wall itself. In 8:8 the root חתר appears twice when the prophet digs a hole in a wall through which he is able to see what is transpiring within. The walls which are mentioned in both chapters 8 and 12 must have been mud brick, through which an opening could have easily been made. Such walls constructed of mud brick were non-existent in the hill country of Palestine in the sixth century B.C. but were the only walls used in house building in Mesopotamia then.

The picture of adobe walls is further reenforced by the vivid description of an old wall in complete disrepair; but instead of rebuilding it workmen covered over its defects with marly clay plaster. A rainstorm washed the plaster away and water penetrated the wall bringing about complete collapse. Had this structure been built of stone a rainstorm certainly could not have destroyed it; but the wall was made of mud brick which was common in Mesopotamia (13:10-15). Substantially the same figure is repeated in Ez. 22:28 leaving no doubt about the structural material used in the walls described by our prophet. They were in fact adobe walls.30

These two objects are factual indications, not conclusions drawn from doubtful premises, that the prophet did his "play acting" in Babylon. A redactor who could make such subtle

alterations in order to give the book a Babylonian dress is
hardly admissible.³¹

One or more redactors are the vehicles by which all difficulties are at last disposed of by those who insist on shifting
the scene from Babylon to Palestine. Kittel has a very timely
warning for those who use this easy way out.

> According to the principles of strict science, we have in
> fact to assume a duplicity or multiplicity of authors in
> the case of a work that is ascribed to an author of this
> sort, only if there is a question of declarations or psy-
> chic events which could not find place in one single con-
> sciousness.³²

Of course everyone admits that there were later editings of the
book, but one wonders how valid it is to assume two authors in
order "to simplify" the complex personality of the prophet. By
positing enough redactors the locale of any literary work could
be easily shifted. Actually to assume so many is subjectivism
at its worst since it permits anyone to superimpose his own
idea of what should have happened upon that which actually did
occur. By using such a method history could be made more order-
ly, less complicated and completely inaccurate.³³

These eight areas of discussion show plainly that the case
for a Palestinian residence is not nearly so strong as it might
appear at first glance. Underlying each point is the unproven
assumption that Ezekiel did not live in Babylon, hence argu-
mentation is a means to substantiate what is already assumed to
be true. Tradition along with many facts which have been and
will be adduced show that the premise is untenable. Next we
must examine additional arguments which appear in individual
works on the subject.

Volkmar Herntrich's case rests primarily on the eight points
which have been examined and discussed above. He leans heavily
upon the Redactor to build his new picture of the book and is
possessed with desire to deliver Ezekiel from the garb of ab-
normality.³⁴ Of course he has no way of knowing details about
the complexity or simplicity of the prophetic personality unless he accepts tradition. Herntrich is concerned with the fact
that our prophet does not mention King Jehoiachin or the conditions under which members of the gôlāh were forced to live.³⁵

> Perhaps Cooke is correct in his explanation of this difficulty.
> Israel's apostasy and the inevitable doom occupied his
> mind to the exclusion of everything else, he had no
> feeling to spare for any hardships of his own and though
> he was not blind to the character of the Babylonians
> (7:21; 12:13; 23:25; 28:7; 30:11), he regarded them as

the instruments of God's purpose and accepted the situation because he knew how to interpret it.36
However, we would be much more inclined to the view that the best part of valor in such a situation was silence. What possible value could a prophetic denunciation of the Chaldeans have either for the exiles in Tel-Abib or for those Jews still living in Jerusalem and Judah? On the one hand it would bring repressive measures by the Chaldean authorities, and on the other it would build up a feeling of self-righteousness among the Jews. In fact, the prophet in making such a denunciation might have been understood as denying the lesson of history which was the main purpose of the whole exilic experience.37 Some try to see Babylon underlying the evil forces portrayed in chapters 38 and 39, but that is very doubtful. It should be pointed out that the whole dating scheme is built with Jehoiachin's captivity in mind; hence, the fact of the king's captivity was not completely neglected unless we are to declare all dates to be inaccurate (see chapter II below). Herntrich presents a well thought out position but probably failed to weigh carefully the traditional view before embarking on his "new picture."

I.G. Matthews' position is not quite so weak as that of Herntrich since he at least admits that the prophet carried on his work somewhere until 570 B.C. Yet Matthews' evidence for a Palestinian locale is inadequate, as we have shown in the general discussion above. His statement that one can make a case for a Phoenician, Israelite or Egyptian residence for the prophet in his latter years on the basis of allusions in the text is not to be seriously considered.38 J.B. Harford holds essentially the same views as Matthews and Herntrich and so must stand or fall with them.39

Bertholet's very excellent and important study of Ezekiel is weakest on the residence problem, which he seeks to solve with a novel three-residence theory. Underlying Bertholet's reconstruction is a feeling that a partial Palestinian setting is necessary to explain the words and actions of our prophet. Already we have indicated that such is not the case. This scholar is the first to our knowledge to propose that chapter 12 represents a real and not a symbolic removal from the doomed city. If indeed the prophet actually left the city, how could he possibly interpret the meaning of such queer activity "in the morning" (12:8)? It is very strange that news of the city's fall should be so long in coming if the prophet were living at the time within Judah's boundaries (33:21).40 Furthermore, one can easily recognise that this part of Bertholet's interpretation is at best a conclusion drawn from exceedingly questionable evidence.41 Auvray's deep concern for the prophet's life if he remained in besieged Jerusalem is misplaced since few populations ever suffered complete extinction even in such a holocaust as that which enveloped Jerusalem in 587 B.C.[42]

By juggling the date in Ez. 1:1 Bertholet arrives at the thirteenth year of Jehoiachin's captivity as the time for Ezekiel's second call to prophecy.[43] The new field of his activity would be Babylon (1:4-2:2). We agree that Ezekiel spent the latter part of his career in Babylon, but exception must be taken to Bertholet's assumption of two earlier abodes.

O.R. Fisher's ideas on residence are the most attractive and at the same time the most logical of those presented by scholars at odds with the traditional position. Although it was possible to make the trip from Tel-Abib to Jerusalem, we doubt that a fugitive such as Ezekiel would long have escaped the long arm of Chaldean authority. Except in a caravan such a trek would be impossible and if in caravan the escapee would have probably been detected. Moreover, it is incredible that one who was probably a leading member of the upper class taken into captivity in 598 B.C. should have been allowed to remain in Jerusalem unmolested for six long years.[44] This solution simplifies our identification of the audiences to which Ezekiel spoke and also clears up several other supposed difficulties; however, there is not one shred of solid evidence for a real return on the part of the prophet to Jerusalem. Somewhere in the book one would expect at least a hint that such a trip was made. Taking Ez. 9 to be a real description of the destruction and looting of fallen Jerusalem is certainly going counter to the obvious apocalyptic style of the passage. This view can be accepted only as a last resort when all other explanations have failed. The book of Ezekiel as it now stands is better explained by a complete Babylonian locale for the work of the prophet.

At this time it is appropriate to point out several references in the text regarding "the Spirit" by which our prophet was reputedly transported from place to place. Herntrich, Matthews, Harford, Bertholet and Fisher have either rejected or neglected these passages thus necessitating the bodily presence of Ezekiel in Jerusalem.

"So the Spirit lifted me up, and took me away; and I went in bitterness in the heat of my spirit. . ." (3:14)

"And the Spirit lifted me up between earth and heaven and brought me in visions of God to Jerusalem." (8:3)

"And the Spirit lifted me up and brought me in the vision by the Spirit of God into Chaldea to them of the captivity." (11:24)

"In the visions of God brought he me unto the land of Israel and set me down upon a very high mountain, whereon was as it were the frame of a city upon the South." (40:2)

Not once does the prophet claim that he went in the flesh to Jerusalem, rather were his trips completely visionary. Further material on the visions of Ezekiel will be presented in chapter IV.

The year 602 B.C. marked the beginning of Ezekiel's prophetic activity, according to Oesterley and Robinson. How they arrived at this specific date is not explained, but the main reason for early dating is a Jewish tradition claiming that Ezekiel prophesied in Palestine before he went to Tel-Abib, which is insufficient evidence for such a radical change in date.[45]

James Smith in reading the book of Ezekiel concluded that Ezekiel was a Northern prophet who lived out part of his ministry in Palestine and the rest among the Jews of the Assyrian diaspora. Taking Smith's arguments one by one, it is rather easy to answer them. His contention that neither Jeremiah nor Kings mentions Ezekiel proves nothing since Ezekiel and Kings do not mention Jeremiah, which would make Jeremiah a fiction.[46] The arguments of this Scottish scholar regarding the gôlāh have been adequately dealt with already. We need not go back to Assyrian times to find exiles among whom he might have lived, nor is it necessary to grant that his message would be irrelevant to Babylonian exiles (cf. above). His view that the Chaldeans, contrary to Assyrian practice, did not require religious submission to the national god is probably incorrect.[47] We shall have occasion to point out in more detail later that Josiah's Reform was not completely successful, as Smith thinks; hence one would expect a reactionary return to pre-Josianic practices, i.e. sun worship, Baal and Astarte cults. We forego discussing Smith's dates here since that is the subject of the next chapter.

Several writers support Smith's idea that Ezekiel was a native of North Israel, but their evidence is extremely weak.[48] Already the term "house of Israel" has been disposed of as possible support for a northern origin. Just as far fetched is Smith's idea that the idolatry described in chapter 6 is more in keeping with the north than with the south. How could he possibly know?[49] The same question might be asked about the statement that the oracles against the false prophets point more to Israel than to Judah. Whether the simile of the vine is northern, southern or neutral, nobody can be sure, but even if it were northern, there is no reason why a later prophet of Judah should not use it, especially since that prophet was in Exile and looked to the day when Israel and Judah would be one nation. Along the same line the tradition of Hittite and Amorite parentage for Jerusalem possibly did begin in the north, but that does not preclude its presence in the oracles of a prophet from Judah. The fact that Ezekiel judges the sin of Judah to be more heinous than that of Israel (Ez. 23) does not prove northern origin because by the same sort of argument one could prove that Ezekiel came from Sodom or Gomorrah, whose sin was also less to his mind than that of Judah. Obviously Smith does not have sufficient evidence to support either a northern origin in the time of Manasseh for the prophet or a ministry among the Jews of the Assyrian diaspora.

At this point it should be apparent to the reader that one can quite logically hold that Ezekiel lived in Babylonia and that accepting any variant view raises more problems than it settles. For example, suppose we accept the view that the book stems not from a prophet living among the gôlâh but rather comes to us in its present form from a redactor who added the Babylonian background and visionary material. Why did the redactor move the locale from Palestine to Babylon? Some of the Babylonian atmosphere in the book is so very subtle that it presupposes in the redactor a remarkable literary skill. Can we assume such sophistication on the part of the redactor? There are many other knotty problems which these variant proposals bring forth.

On the other hand, a Babylonian residence for the prophet eliminates the need for one or more redactors and does not, as we shall see later, necessitate clairvoyance on the part of the prophet. Ezekiel's messages by natural channels most assuredly found their way back to Judah and Jerusalem. Each of the oracles was more or less relevant to the exiles in Tel-Abib as a future warning. Experiences of the prophet within Jerusalem are clearly marked as visions and should be taken as nothing more. Most problems can be solved by assuming a Babylonian background for all the prophet's work.

There are a few more positive points which can be used as evidence favoring a Mesopotamian setting for the prophecy. The name Judah appears in Ezekiel only thirteen times; but in the contemporary work of Jeremiah the same term is used in all connections 169 times. Israel is found 183 times in Ezekiel but occurs only about 100 times in Jeremiah. From this evidence it may be concluded that the name Judah had far less significance for Ezekiel than for Jeremiah, a fact which can easily be explained if we accept Ezekiel as the prophet who lived among the captives. Since Jeremiah was still resident in Judah, he could hardly be expected to neglect the name; but with a prophet in Exile the case was different. He looked for the restoration not of Judah alone but of all Israel. It was probably for this reason that he used the term Israel, the chosen of God, in reference to his people; but, as we have seen above, the name has no one specific meaning in the book. There is no doubt that the prophet used the name Israel to indicate the people who would be restored and who would receive God's favor (cf. 20:40-44; 37:11, in chapters 38-39). Usage of these terms then indicates clearly that the author of the book bearing the name Ezekiel lived outside Palestine.

Chapter III of this dissertation deals in detail with the language of the prophecy, but it might be well to point out here that there is substantial linguistic evidence for a Babylonian setting. Formerly Aramaisms were taken as an indication of a very late date for any work in which they were detected; but, as we shall see below, that judgment is not always correct.

Again we must hold off our main exposition of the prophet's visionary life for a later chapter where it properly comes. By way of preview, it may be said that the visions of Ezekiel are expected from a man of delicate temperament living in such distressing times. There are remarkable parallels between Ezekiel and great mystics of many faiths, a point which we shall discuss at another time.

Several scholars have doubted the reality of the place Tel-Abib.[50] However, it now turns out that the name Tel-Abib and the canal Chebar add force to the case for a Babylonian locale. Tel-Abib is probably to be identified with <u>til abūb</u>, meaning "primordial mound." The Babylonian word refers to the low mounds of long destroyed towns in Mesopotamia which were thought to date prior to the Flood; abubu means "deluge."
אביב is a natural Hebrew scribal adaptation of אבוב in view of the month "Abib." On one of these sites it would be possible for a colony to live once the irrigation works were repaired. Needless to say, such mounds did not appear in Palestine. Parallel names are later listed in Ezra and Nehemiah when mention is made of the exilic settlements at Tel-Melah and Tel-Harsha. Similar names never appeared prior to the Exile. As for the River Chebar, that too has long since been identified with the canal <u>Kabar</u> near Nippur, mentioned frequently in cuneiform

documents from the Persian period. These place names fit perfectly into the geographical and chronological context that tradition claims for our prophet.[51]

Finally, the author of Ez. 48 certainly was not within the borders of Palestine else we would have no such ideal geometric divisions of the land as are found in this picture of the future. The country lay in shambles when these words were written. Under such conditions it was possible for a prophet not living in the ruined land to reapportion it among the tribes in a plan for the time of restoration.

The most adequate explanation of the Ezekiel residence problem is found in the centuries-old traditional view that he was a prophet to the Babylonian gôlāh. This explanation does not solve all the difficulties, but it explains more and raises fewer than any other one so far proposed.

Objections to the traditional view at first seem to be insurmountable, but on closer examination they prove to be rather minor. There is no major reason why Ezekiel could not have been a captive in 598 B.C. who was called to prophesy five years later at a place called Tel-Abib in Mesopotamia. Nor is there cause for abandoning the belief, founded on strong evidence, that the prophet spent the rest of his life among the captives in Babylon. We need not use clairvoyance as an explanation of the visionary phenomena contained in the book, for they can properly be understood as ordinary psychic experiences of a highly sensitive soul.

The variant theories rest on two assumptions neither of which is valid or tenable. First, it is assumed that the traditional Babylonian locale is passé and can no longer be intelligently maintained. Along with this first premise goes a second like it, namely, that a Palestinian residence is true, hence we must seek evidence to prove what is self-evident. Neither premise has been or can be proven.

Positive pieces of evidence for a Babylonian locale include the לבנה of 4:1 and the mud brick walls of chapters 8, 12, 13:10-15 and 22:28. Both of these facts are clear indications that the prophet was in Babylon. The use of the term Israel in Ezekiel almost to the exclusion of Judah is further proof that the prophet was not within the bounds of his native land. Explanation of the name Tel-Abib along with the identification of the River Chebar lend further support to a Babylonian setting.

The inability of scholars to produce a theory superior to

the traditional view plus the extremely strong evidence for the long accepted position shows clearly that no change is needed in our interpretation of Ezekiel as far as residence is concerned.

Ezekiel was the prophet of the gōlāh at Tel-Abib, where he received his call; and it was among his fellow captives in Babylon that he carried out his entire mission.

Chapter II

THE DATE OF THE PROPHECY

LIKE EZEKIEL'S RESIDENCE, the date of his prophecy has been seriously questioned only in comparatively recent times. For centuries it was assumed that tradition was correct in dating the beginning of the prophet's work about 593 B.C., five years after the beginning of Jehoiachin's Babylonian captivity, when he saw a magnificent vision and received the call to prophesy from Yahweh. The dates in the remainder of the book, all fourteen of them, were accepted as being accurate and were never doubted by ancient Jewish or Christian commentators. As we shall see later, the troublesome "thirtieth year" (1:1) gave rise to some difficulty, but otherwise the oracles of Ezekiel could be dated more exactly than those of any other prophet known in Jewish tradition. The prophet of the gôlāh exercised his ministry between 593 B.C. (1:2) and 571 B.C. (29:17).

L. Zunz was the first important scholar to challenge the entire dating system in Ezekiel, taking it to be artificial. After considerable study, he gave the opinion that the prophecy is definitely set in the Persian period, more precisely between 440-400 B.C. Chapters 26-28 are placed even later since in them is portrayed Alexander's conquest of Tyre in 332 B.C.[1]

Seinecke's fanciful Maccabean dating has been discussed above, and E. Havet's identification of the Temple in chapters 40-48 with that of Herod is not worthy of consideration. Winckler places most of the prophecy between 539-515 B.C., and C.R. Berry would make the book pre-Maccabean.[2] We shall have occasion later in the chapter to note more in detail Berry's dating of Ezekiel.

The most radical and revolutionary proposal on the question of date was submitted by C.C. Torrey in his Pseudo-Ezekiel. Torrey takes the book of Ezekiel to be a pseudepigraphon, based on II Kgs. 21:2-16 and written about 230 B.C. with a Palestinian setting. The prophecy is a historical novel concerning the times of Manasseh. Ezekiel, the man, never existed. Before 200 B.C. the pseudepigraphon had been revised and given a Babylonian setting by a writer whose primary aim was to prove that Yahweh could speak outside the boundaries of Palestine proper.[3]

Torrey begins his case with the assertion that the doubt about canonization of the book (see above) rested not on disagreement between the Tôrāh and legal sections of Ezekiel, as Jewish tradition claims, but had a more subtle source. Further, the author of Pseudo-Ezekiel does not take seriously the Jewish concern over theosophical speculation in connection with chapter 1. He points out that while chapter 1 was proscribed for youths under thirty and for reading in the synagogue, no such proscription was placed against chapter 10, which contains essentially the same vision. Torrey maintains that the authorities responsible for canonization of the prophecy knew that the work was not composed by an Ezekiel of the Babylonian gôlāh, for according to him, Jewish tradition knows no such prophet. The work was of such extraordinary interest, bearing within itself the marks of true prophecy and high religion, that its rejection would have been a terrible loss to Judaism. So the Jews threw up a smoke screen against possible detection of the truth by some alert mind. In order to deceive future readers the Jews expressed grave concern over the legal differences between Ezekiel on the one hand and the Tôrāh on the other. Also, the Jews expressed fear that Ez. 1 would lead to dangerous theosophical speculations. According to Torrey, the differences between regulations in the Temple Law and the Ideal Temple Law of Ezekiel were of no concern to the Jews because one was for the present, the other for the future.[4]

Pseudo-Ezekiel is supported further by the belief that the prophet was speaking to people who lived in Palestine. No reference is made to the living conditions of the Babylonian gôlāh, and the people among whom Ezekiel actually lived, unlike captives, had enough to eat. It is unbelievable, according to Torrey, that a group of Jewish exiles without organization or subsidization could have survived in Babylonia. Adduced also as added material against a Babylonian locale is the place name Tel-Abib, which is said not to be Babylonian.[5]

The Pseudo-Ezekiel structure rests heavily on the contention that Josiah's Reform was completely successful, hence all syncretism described in the prophecy would be pre-Josianic. Torrey is certain about this alleged fact, as shown by the following: "The reform of Josiah was successful and its effect lasting, as would long ago have been established but for the confusion which the Babylonian Editor of Ezekiel has introduced."[6]

Moloch worship, which supposedly passed from the scene during the Josianic Reform is further proof that Ezekiel is fiction, according to Torrey.[7]

The failure on the part of our prophet to mention the presence of Jeremiah on the contemporary scene plus the statement

THE DATE OF THE PROPHECY   29

by Ezekiel that there were no prophets in Judah (22:25, 28, 30) provide further grist for the Pseudo-Ezekiel mill. Torrey explains this by claiming that Jeremiah actually had not appeared in the historical era which forms the background for Ezekiel. Yet he insists that Ezekiel is literally dependent on Jeremiah, a point which would, if true, provide further evidence for a pseudepigraphical work.[8]

The mention of Paras (27:10; 38:5) long before the Persians appeared as a factor in ancient history is a strong element pointing, Torrey thinks, to a late date for composition of the book. Along with this fact is the exact description of a Persian religious rite (according to Torrey) in Ez. 8:17, which necessitates revision of the historical setting of the prophecy.[9]

Torrey makes much of the Aramaic in the book, using this as a strong argument for his late dating. This plus the many affinities with the Priestly material of the Pentateuch clinches the case for Pseudo-Ezekiel to the mind of its author.[10]

A specific date for the composition of the prophecy as we have it now is determined, according to Torrey, by comparison with the book of Daniel. Ez. 31:5f, 10, 12b, 13 is dependent on Daniel 4:7-14, which was composed about 245 B.C. In Ez. 14: 14, 20 Daniel is mentioned, presupposing that Ezekiel was familiar with at least a primitive form of the book which bears Daniel's name. The first six chapters of Daniel were manifestly written during the time of the war between the Seleucids and the Ptolemies, the most probable date being during the war between Antiochus II and Ptolemy III. At this time the Seleucids would most closely resemble the clay portion while the Ptolemies could be correctly likened unto the iron section of the image described in Daniel. This would peg the early book of Daniel about 240 B.C. Since the prophecy of Ezekiel is first mentioned in Ben Sira (180 B.C.), our book should be placed somewhere between the two dates. Torrey chooses 230 B.C. as the date for the original pseudepigraphon, which had a Palestinian locale. Before 200 B.C., however, the book was completely revised by the "Babylonian Redactor," who invented the whole Babylonian scheme of things.[11]

Closely akin to the theory of Pseudo-Ezekiel is the work of James Smith, which has been discussed at some length above. Our prophet, according to Smith, came from the North; most of his ministry was spent in Palestine, but he did speak also among the exiles of the Assyrian diaspora (not Babylonian). With Torrey, Smith argues that the religious situation described by the prophet must be pre-Josianic since the reform of that king was probably completely successful. The most likely time for such syncretistic, idolatrous worship would be the age of Manasseh. Lack of information on the gōlāh and the failure of Jeremiah to mention Ezekiel are added arguments, according to Smith, for a change in date. All lines of evidence converge, as far as Smith is concerned, to establish beyond reasonable doubt that our prophet lived during the reign of Manasseh, prophesied partly in Palestine and partly in the Jewish diaspora of Manasseh's times. The two groups of oracles were later united by the Redactor, who superimposed upon the book a Babylonian locale and a sixth century date.[12]

Nils Messel also substantially alters the traditional date of the prophecy, assigning a post-Nehemiah setting to the book. According to Messel, the time of Ezekiel is about 400 B.C. while that of the Redactor is to be set at 350 B.C.[13]

A closer look at Torrey's logical, well-thought-out hypothesis reveals that it rests upon faulty premises and that the evidence drawn in its support no longer holds. The positing of Pseudo-Ezekiel is a necessary corollary of a theory long held by Torrey and his followers, namely, that the Babylonian Exile was a rather unimportant ripple on the sea of Jewish history. There was no catastrophic destruction of the cities of Judah by the Chaldeans, and the population was not deported en masse to Babylonia. That there was devastation and a minor exile is not denied by Torrey, but he will not admit that the restoration of the Jewish nation took place through the return of these Babylonian exiles.[14] This whole restoration theme rests, according to him, on fabrications of the Chronicler, who is in no case to be trusted. Quoting Torrey directly here would be wise since on occasion he has thought himself "misrepresented."

> If any of the villages and cities of Judea were much depopulated, it was certainly for a short time only.[15]

> After the Chaldean invasion the portions of the city which were left vacant or thinned out be deportation, conflagration, and the exodus due to fear and discouragement were eventually reoccupied not only by Jews but also by companies of foreign immigrants. This was doubtless true also of the Judean villages which had been wholly or partially abandoned.[16]

Archeology has lately become the bitter foe of Torrey's views, for the facts which this science has produced makes it difficult to reconstruct history according to a prearranged plan. Running directly counter to Torrey's reconstruction of the state of affairs in Judah following the Chaldean conquest is the fact that many towns were completely destroyed at that time and never reoccupied. Albright twenty years ago listed the following places as sites definitely occupied in the seventh century B.C. but showing no signs of reoccupation in post-Exilic times: Tell-el-Ḥuweilifeh, Tell ʿAiṭûn, Tell ed-Duweir (Lachish), Tell ed-Djudeideh, Tell Zakariya (Azekah), Ḥirbet ʿAbbâd (Socho), Ḥirbet eš-šeiḥ Madkûr (Adullam), Tell Qîlā (Keilah) and others. To this list may be added Tell Beit Mirsim and Beth-Shemesh, whose destruction can be placed during Nebuchadrezzar's campaign against Zedekiah. Azekah and Lachish (Jer. 34: 6-7) were the last fortified sites which held out with Jerusalem against the Chaldean attack; hence the end of their occupation can be set approximately contemporaneous with the fall of Jerusalem. Archeological fact leaves no doubt about the complete destruction left in the wake of the Babylonian conquest of Judah.[17]

Torrey's ingenious explanation of canonization difficulties is completely refuted by S. Spiegel in his "Ezekiel or Pseudo-Ezekiel." The claim that the rabbis knew that Ezekiel was a pseudepigraphon and accepted it carries in any case little conviction. As Spiegel correctly points out:

> Had the least doubt prevailed as to the authenticity of Ezekiel would it not have been more natural to indicate, if only by the subtlest hints, that its testimony does not deserve equal weight with the rest of sacred scriptures. The earnestness with which the ritual deviations are discussed, the assiduity employed in harmonizing them with the Law of Moses, bespeak rather the underlying belief in the genuineness of Ezekiel.[18]

Many times the rabbis busied themselves in trying to harmonize Ezekiel and the Tôrāh. For example, Ez. 46:6 prescribes that the burnt offering at the time of the new moon should consist of one young bullock and six lambs, but Numbers 28:11 requires two bullocks and seven lambs for the same occasion. This inconsistency has been set right in the following manner:

> It teaches that if one cannot find two bullocks, he may offer one; if he cannot bring seven lambs, he may offer six. Yea, even if he cannot bring five, he may bring four, or lacking four, three; or lacking three, two, even one, for it is written: And for the lambs according as his hand shall attain unto. . .Ez. 46:7. (Menahoth 45a)[19]

How strange it is that the rabbis would be constantly bothered by a prophecy which was known to be a pseudepigraphon!

The opinion, expressed by Torrey, that the Law of the Ideal

Temple was for the future age and the Mosaic Law was for immediate practice shows a complete misunderstanding of the Jewish concept of the Law. There was but one Law which existed before the world was, would continue as long as the world lasted and would be just as binding in the Messianic Age as before.[20]

Torrey's belief that Jewish tradition knew no Ezekiel of the gôlāh is erroneous. There are references to this prophet of Yahweh, who dwelt without the bounds of Palestine proper, even though a Palestinian residence would have been more in keeping with current belief. One story is related by Jewish tradition concerning the funeral of a great leader who had lived outside the Holy Land. In a eulogy to the deceased a speaker expressed his sorrow that the deceased had been unable to attain true greatness on account of his foreign residence whereupon an individual in the audience shouted in reply, "And the word of the Lord came unto Ezekiel in Babylon."[21]

But let us look at the tradition which leads Torrey to doubt an Ezekielian authorship. In Baba Bathra 14b-15a it is stated that: "The Men of the Great Assembly wrote. . .Ezekiel, the Twelve Minor Prophets, Daniel and the Scroll of Esther." (Baba Bathra 15a)[22] However in the same passage the Pentateuch is assigned to Moses, while Joshua is the author of the book bearing his name and Samuel is given credit for two books of the same name along with Judges and Ruth. Jeremiah is reputed to have written not only his own book but Kings and Lamentations as well; and the colleagues of Hezekiah are responsible for Isaiah, Proverbs, Song of Songs and Ecclesiastes. We are astonished that Torrey would give so much weight to a source which is probably fourth century A.D. in date and completely uncritical in approach.[23]

Already we have had occasion to show how the prophet could be in Babylon and yet speak to the people of Jerusalem as well as those among whom he lived. Reason for neglecting to describe the conditions under which the captives lived has also been explained. Torrey is simply wrong in saying that Tel-Abib is not Babylonian (see above). Since these points have all been reviewed earlier in this study, we shall pass on to other factors which are used as evidence in Torrey's case.[24]

Basic to the theory of Pseudo-Ezekiel is the claim that Josiah's Reform was completely successful in blotting out the religious syncretism typical of the Manasseh era. The way in which Torrey gets rid of contrary evidence is amazing. Jehoiakim did "that which was evil in the sight of Yahweh, according to all that his fathers had done" (II Kgs. 23:37); Jehoiachin likewise is accused of having done "that which was evil in the sight of Yahweh, according to all his father had done" (II Kgs. 24:9), and Zedekiah is judged for committing "that which was evil in the sight of Yahweh, according to all Jehoiachin had done" (II Kgs. 24:19). But according to Torrey these statements are "stereotyped phrase." II Chronicles 36:14 pictures people practicing "the abominations of the nations" and polluting the Temple so the verse is dismissed as "a homiletical improvement," and the testimony of Is. 57:5 regarding child sacrifice is said to have no real bearing on the case as Torrey sees it. Jer. 7: 31 is assigned to an earlier reign, Jer. 19:5 is denied to the prophet Jeremiah and Jer. 32:35 refers to the sins of Judah under Manasseh, although the prophet says that these sins were being committed "even unto this day." Having disposed of these bothersome references in summary fashion, it is proven beyond question that the material in Ezekiel concerning idolatry could not be post-Josianic.[25] Spiegel acidly comments: "Such wholesale massacre of all undesirable witnesses cannot but suggest the failure both of Josiah's reform and of the new interpretation of Ezekiel."[26] By using the same high-handed critical method evident at all times in Pseudo-Ezekiel any scholar could make historical material fall into a pre-arranged framework.

From a practical standpoint one would definitely expect a reaction against the Josianic Reform once the royal leader was dead. If there were no such popular reaction recorded, then the student of history would be safe even then in assuming that such a reactionary movement would follow. In all history one is able to see action and reaction. An important case of historical reaction would be the Counter Reformation which followed the Reformation almost as the seasons follow one another. We believe that Torrey overlooked this extremely significant fact in claiming that Manasseh-like religious activity could have no place in post-Josianic times.

How effective the Reform was is known neither to Torrey or to anybody else; but that complete success was met in what was an official, not a popular reform, is beyond belief. The Reform was undoubtedly the most thoroughgoing which Judah had ever experienced, and it must have quickly driven the unorthodox underground, where they waited for a chance to reassert themselves. According to the record, as it stood before Torrey did his work, these practices reappeared, and these worshipers reasserted themselves (Ez. 6:1-10; 8:1-17; Jer. 19 and elsewhere). Such a reformation could not last long without heavy popular support, which was lacking in this case.

The mention of Paras in Ez. 27:10, 38:5 and Dan'el in Ez.14:

14, 20 are strong reasons as far as Torrey is concerned for making a sixth century B.C. date impossible. The Weidner tablets from Babylon, which are dated 592 B.C. and in which Persians are mentioned, dispose of the first argument completely.[27] Persians were very much on the scene of history by Ezekiel's time. As for Dan'el (note the difference in spelling from Daniel) every student of the Bible should be familiar with the Ras Shamra (Ugarit) Dan'el. Since this individual is grouped with such ancient figures as Noah and Job, it is incredible that he should be the Daniel of the Babylonian captivity. The great Dan'el figure of Ras Shamra literature fits perfectly into the trio of ancient righteous men.[28]

The argument that Aramaic in Ezekiel indicates a very late date requires serious attention.[29] In our next chapter we expect to show that the Aramaic of Ezekiel, far from forcing the objective student to abandon a sixth century B.C. setting for the prophecy, is actually further evidence for the traditional dating of the book.

Discussion of the so-called Priestly and other late literary material is a complicated and delicate matter. The last few years have proven the dates in Burrows' "The Literary Relations of Ezekiel to be all but completely inaccurate. Beyond question this dating of Old Testament sources originated with Torrey.[30]

Pseudo-Ezekiel is the clever creation, not of a Jewish novelist of the third century B.C., but of a professor of the twentieth century A.D. It is a well-worked-out theory which rests on false premises and is supported throughout by inconclusive evidence.

Much in the same vein is James Smith's reinterpretation of the prophet's life and work. It is to Smith's credit that he admits the possibility of a popular religious reaction against the official reform of Josiah, but in the admission his case is damaged considerably.[31] Both his and Torrey's argument that Ezekiel's and Jeremiah's ignoring each other is a proof that Ezekiel was not a contemporary of Jeremiah is fallacious, as we have seen above.[32]

In dealing with the date of the prophecy we must at the same time discuss the fourteen dates which appear in the text. Some have accepted them completely at face value while others deny them completely and still others accept those which fit their own particular point of view.

Torrey's treatment of the dates is extremely interesting

THE DATE OF THE PROPHECY

since he is able to make them fit into the reign of Manasseh. This remarkable feat is accomplished by examining the "thirtieth year" in Ez. 1:1, which must refer to the thirtieth year of the reign of some king. That king would necessarily have to be pre-Josianic since religious conditions described in the book no longer existed after the successful reform of Josiah. What king of the seventh century B.C. reigned thirty years or more? Only one answer is possible, Manasseh, who is said to have reigned fifty-five years. Then Torrey makes a startling discovery: "...the months and days exhibit a regular sequence of their own, quite irrespective of the years to which they are assigned in our present text."[33] Then he proceeds to the conclusion that the years are "one and all false" thus paving the way for a complete dating scheme in Manasseh's reign. Starting in Ez. 1:1 with the thirtieth year, the fourth month and the fifth day, Torrey builds a perfect chronological sequence of Manasseh dates down through Ez. 40:1, which is the thirty-fifth year, the first month and the tenth day.[34] The assumption of the era of Manasseh as the historical backdrop is the basis for this revision of dates.

Unique among explanations of the dates contained in the prophecy is that of James Smith, who when he cannot make a particular reference fit into a given dating scheme seeks another system of dating. While admitting that Smith's efforts in this respect are of dubious value, a presentation of his results would at least be instructive.

Smith thinks he detects in the prophet's work as we now have it the use of three distinct dating systems, namely, Assyrian dating, dating by Jewish kings and a dating from the captivity of Tiglath-pileser III in 734 B.C. "The twelfth year of our captivity" (33:21) is to be counted from 734 B.C. when Tiglath-pileser carried out his partial deportation of the inhabitants of Dan and Naphtali giving 722 B.C., which is the date when Samaria was captured. Samaria, not Jerusalem, must have been the "smitten city" since the general situation portrayed is a clear picture of the prevailing conditions following the fall of the northern capital city.[36] In this same dating system the ninth year (24:1) is also to be placed since it is the ninth year of the captivity (725 B.C.).[37]

"The twenty-fifth year of our captivity...in the fourteenth year after the city was smitten" is 709-8 B.C. when Sargon had begun to rebuild the waste places. This official reconstruction program gave rise to Ezekiel's contemplation of a new Temple of the future.[38]

36   THE DATE AND COMPOSITION OF EZEKIEL

Without wasting too much time on this fantastic chronological reconstruction, we briefly present Smith's ideas about the remaining dates. The thirtieth year in Ez. 1:1 is the thirtieth year (according to Smith's chronology) after Samaria was destroyed, which turns out to be the fifth year of Manasseh's rule (692 B.C.).

The dates in 8:1, 26:1, 29:1, 30:20, 32:1 are definitely, Smith holds, dates according to the reign of Esarhaddon, king of Assyria. In the sixth year of Esarhaddon (676/5 B.C.) he says that the Assyrians conquered Jerusalem. The twenty-seventh year in 29:17 is a second date from the reign of Manasseh which is synchronized with the Assyrian dating of the same chapter. It was in the eleventh year of Esarhaddon (30:21) when the arm of Egypt was broken and in his twelfth year most of the threats against the empire of the Nile were fulfilled. So Smith concludes that Ezekiel's main work was carried out between 725 and 669 B.C.[39] It is not necessary to point out to the careful reader that any scholar by using enough different dating systems can successfully shift the dates of any composition if that scholar is sufficiently arbitrary in the way he treats facts.

Irwin's work on The Problem of Ezekiel will be carefully examined in chapter V, but it would be of value to present his disposal of the dates at this juncture. Perhaps the reader should be reminded that by "an inductive" method Irwin reduces the book to 251 verses in part or in their entirety. The discussion of dates by Irwin starts out with the statement that 33:21 is obviously the work of the "Babylonian editor," 40:1 is definitely spurious, while 8:1, 32:1 and 32:17 are certainly incorrect. There is much uncertainty about 31:1, and 1:2 is nothing but a "harmonistic gloss." Irwin concedes that the dates in 24:1, 29:17 and 26:1 are correct, whereas those in 29:1, 30:20 and 20:1 may possibly be accurate. But in 20:1 the date is followed by the verb בא appropriate to a visit of the elders instead of usual היה. Such a definite variant naturally makes this date spurious. Again a mixup in the usual introductory formula in 29:1, which begins "in the tenth year" as over against the normal "it came to pass," suggests that the hand of the Redactor has been at work. The usual order is reversed in 24:1, where the announcement of the revelation is placed before the date which, according to criteria arrived at by "induction," could not possibly come from Ezekiel but must have its source elsewhere.[40]

Finally Irwin reaches the following amazing conclusion which deserves direct quotation: "Fully half the dates are clearly spurious: what basis is there for granting special consideration to the other half?"[41] The dates found in 29:1, 17 and 30: 20 are taken to be correct, providing valuable information about the date of Pharaoh Hophra's intervention on behalf of the Jews in Palestine; however, the correctness of these dates does not necessitate their having originated with the prophet. On the contrary, Irwin is certain that they are to be traced to the Babylonian Editor.[42]

Since the wording of 20:1 is slightly different from the other dates, Irwin declares that it is so far uniform with the group as to carry the implication of a common origin. The only date to be seriously considered is "the thirtieth year" in Ez. 1:1, which refers to the age of the prophet. This strange date is unique but is also spurious. So much for the dates as far as Irwin is concerned.[43] His whole work stands or falls with the validity of his approach, which we shall examine closely in chapter V.

G.R. Berry held that the dates are all editorial. Some rest on genuine, accurate tradition while others are plainly in error. In a partial analysis of the work Berry claims that Ez. 18 with its doctrine of individualism is too far advanced for the sixth century B.C. An element of exaggeration in chapter 19 indicates a late date. All the oracles of hope along with those passages couched in apocalyptic language are manifestly late in composition. Oracles against the neighbors of Judah came about 450 B.C., but the chapters on Tyre are to be placed about 300 B.C., and the oracle against Egypt (Ez. 29-30) is dated 350 B.C. In other words, Berry admits a genuine core of Palestinian oracles spoken by a real Ezekiel, but the book as we now have it is an edition of the third century B.C. which sketched in the Babylonian setting and added chapters 40-48.[44] We see no necessity for a thoroughgoing discussion of Berry's material since much of it must be discounted in view of facts already presented. However, it is impossible to demonstrate that the individualism of Ez. 18 is a late development. We should remind ourselves that ideas such as this doctrine of individualism do not suddenly appear full grown from nowhere in post-Exilic times without some previous historical development. Once the body politic was destroyed in Judah and social organization was disrupted, the traditional group thinking of the Hebrews naturally gave way more and more to the individualistic approach reflected in Ez. 18. That we submit is what took place among the exiles, whose situation provides a perfect breeding ground for such new and radical ideas.

We have yet to understand either why apocalyptic style on

the one hand or prophecies of hope on the other must be given a late date. It has been known for some time now that in Egypt there were prophecies going back to the Twelfth Dynasty (cir. 2000-1800 B.C.) in which doom and hope were balanced.[45]

I.G. Matthews contends that the well arranged dating system is the product of editorial activity and is a framework which has been superimposed upon the prophecy. He thinks that these dates show strong Babylonian influence and are probably relatively accurate. Citing several examples, Matthews argues that many "individual oracles" are really composite, hence no one date can possibly be correct for all the material following it. Unquestionably he is at least partially correct in saying that an oracle as such would hardly be dated and that the dates seem often to have no necessary connection with material following them. Matthews' position has much in it that commends itself to us. Especially valuable is the reminder of the composite character of prophetic writings and the lack of direct connection between the dates and the material between them.[46]

Since none of these attempts to explain the dates of Ezekiel has met with real success, we must examine the material first hand. There is no reason to doubt the relative accuracy of the system even though we are forced to agree with Matthews and Smith (see above) that not all the material found between two given dates necessarily belongs there chronologically. We propose that the dates furnish a key to the composition of the prophecy, but full explanation of the idea will be postponed until chapter V.

A good case can be made for the contention that the dates all originate directly or indirectly from the prophet. On one occasion Ezekiel received the following command from Yahweh: "Son of man, write thee the name of the day, even this selfsame day: the King of Babylon drew close unto Jerusalem this selfsame day." (24:2) Important dates of national or personal significance were most probably recorded by our prophet. But do all the dates refer to major events? The prophetic call is dated in 1:2; 8:1 marks his first visionary trip back to Jerusalem; 20:1 is the date when the "elders of Israel" paid him a visit; 24:1 is the date of the attack on Jerusalem and probably the time when the prophet's wife died. As for the dates in the Tyre and Egypt oracles, they mark the predictions of the overthrow of major sea and land powers in the ancient world. Needless to say, any prophet or political observer would remember the time of oracles against such important states. Of course, the fall of Jerusalem is a date that has never been forgotten, so its presence in 33:21 is rather expected. The most convincing date

is the fourteenth anniversary of that same destructive event
(40:1). What better time than this for the prophet to have his
vision of the land restored! These dates occur in connection
with great events both personal and national, hence they would
come much more naturally from Ezekiel than from some later
scribe.

The dates are probably not all correct as they presently
stand in the MT. LXX and Syriac change the twelfth year in 32:1
to the eleventh year. This variant reading should be accepted,
for in this way the proper sequence would be restored to the
Egyptian oracles. Also in the case of 33:21 we read the eleventh year rather than the twelfth year which is found in the
MT. This is not a radical change when one realizes how similar
the two readings look in unpointed Hebrew.
   MT שתי עשרי
  Albright's Revision עשתי (עשתה) עשרי
The loss of one consonant was the origin of this mistake and by
replacing that letter the original date is revived. This emendation would solve the elapse of eighteen months between the
Fall of Jerusalem and the news of that event reaching Babylonia
by reducing the time required for the trip from eighteen to
less than six months. It might well have taken a fugitive six
months to find his way to the Jewish colony at Tel-Abib, but
not eighteen months. Except for these corrections, the dates
are accurate and are from Ezekiel as they now stand.

As we have already hinted, the real enigma of the prophecy
is found in the first verse where reference is made to "the
thirtieth year" without further clarification. Since the dating
system involved here is not known, the field is wide open for
all sorts of interpretations. Presumably the most widely held
explanation is that this date refers to the thirtieth year after Josiah's Reform. The Targum, Jerome, Herrmann, Hölscher and
Louis Finkelstein are only a few of the scholars ancient and
modern to accept this interpretation. A second very popular
view has been that we have here represented the age of the
prophet Ezekiel. As unusual as this personal birth date would
be it has been given support by K. Budde, J.A. Bewer, O. Eissfeldt and many others.[48] Various emendations of the text have
been attempted such as Bertholet's reading "thirteenth" and
Herntrich's preference for "third."[49] Torrey and Smith, as we
have already had occasion to mention, fit the date into Manasseh's times.[50]

Cooke finds a key to the date in the month and day which
follow "the thirtieth year" in verse 1 and "the fifth year" in
verse 2. The "fifth day of the month" is the same in both in-

stances, but in verse 2 the specific month is lacking. It is assumed by Cooke that the month which has dropped out of the present text was also the same in the two verses, leading him to conclude that the two dates are identical but are based on systems which differ by exactly twenty-five years.51

The newest attempt at unraveling "the thirtieth year" puzzle was proposed by Snaith in 1948. According to his article, the "datum line" for the book is 615 B.C., which was the year of Jehoiachin's birth, making the young monarch eighteen years old in 597 B.C. as he is reported to have been in II Kgs. 24:1. Thus 585 B.C. would be the year when the king had reached his thirtieth birthday. Snaith sees several advantages in his explanation. For example, it would place the oracles against Egypt in 604 B.C. giving them a direct connection with the battle of Carchemish. The dates in 8:1 and 20:1 would be moved from the period between 597 B.C. and 586 B.C. to 608 B.C. and 607 B.C.52 respectively. Snaith likes this shift because: "The dates are close upon the untimely death of King Josiah, that untoward event which involved the complete collapse of the religious reformation and the return to all the cults of Canaan."53 There is a second "datum line," 597 B.C. used in 24:1, 26:1, 29:17, 33:21, 40:1 and 1:2. The problem is solved to Snaith's satisfaction by the use of two synchronizable dating systems.54

Underlying most of the attempts to explain the unusual date in 1:1 is a feeling that it must be synchronized with "the fifth year" mentioned in verse 2. It was for this reason that Josiah's Reform was quickly pounced upon as a "datum line," for if one takes 623/2 B.C. as the time when the Reform began and subtracts thirty years therefrom, the result is 593/2 B.C. This date also fits perfectly the fifth year after the 598/7 B.C. exile of Jehoiachin. However, this tendency to force synchronization has given rise to an explanation without parallel in the Bible. Had such an unusual "datum line" been employed it unquestionably would have been explained.

A very convenient method of synchronizing the dates is to assume that 1:1 is calculated from the birth of Ezekiel, but again such a dating has no parallel; hence if it were employed, an explanation would be expected. Snaith's hypothesis suffers from the same fault, for we know of not a single case in ancient Israelite or any other history where dates are marked relative to the king's birthday. The view contributes absolutely nothing to a clarification of the Ezekielian chronology and is at best a guess.55

Since there is no explanation of the dating system lying be-

THE DATE OF THE PROPHECY 41

hind "the thirtieth year," it can be safely concluded that a scribe writing this verse assumed that to his readers the system would be self-evident. Certainly dating by the Josianic Reform, the age of the prophet or the age of Jehoiachin would not be known to any but the most intimate friends of the prophet himself. What "datum line" would be self-evident? The dating system used in the remaining portions of the book is the correct answer. Because "the thirtieth year" was in the regular dating system, no explanation seemed necessary. Therefore, none was given.

How then are we to explain the failure of this date in verse 1 to synchronize with the date in verse 2? No synchronization is necessary because the two dates are different although they come from the same dating system. As Spiegel, Albright and others suggest, this date is the time when Ezekiel's oracles were recorded or published.56 It is not surprising that the day and perhaps the month in the first two dates should be the same since the publication of the prophecy possibly came on the exact anniversary of the prophetic call as well as thirty years after the Exile. Full discussion of this whole hypothesis will be taken up later in chapter V. We conclude therefore that the thirtieth year is in the regular dating scheme and is not to be synchronized with verse 2.

Why did not Ezekiel date, as was customary, according to the regnal years of the king? The employment of a dating system based on the regnal years of a deposed king would almost surely have been considered an act of implied rebellion against Babylon since Zedekiah was king as far as the Chaldeans were concerned (II Kgs. 24:18, Ez. 17:12-14). Jehoiachin's reign lasted only three months before he was forced to surrender and go into captivity (II Kgs. 24:8-17). The fact that Jehoiachin's reign and captivity began in the same year would hardly have escaped notice by the exiled Jews. By dating events with relation to the captivity of Jehoiachin a perfect record of the regnal years of the king was kept without incurring the displeasure of Chaldean authority. This dating would be correct with reference to the then standard post-dating system, in which the accession of the king was reckoned from the first of Nisan following, and since this date would coincide perfectly with the date of his captivity. The addition of the word בגלה made the system quite acceptable to the Chaldeans.57

Moreover the Chaldeans continued to recognize Jehoiachin as the legitimate ruler of the Jews even though he was their captive. Zedekiah was but a puppet who ruled at the sufferance of the Neo-Babylonian empire. After thirty-seven years in prison

Jehoiachin was released and treated as a king by Evil-merodach (II Kgs. 25:27-30). Supporting this Biblical testimony is evidence from the Weidner tablets, discovered at Babyon. Payments of rations "for Jehoiachin, the king of the land of Judah, and for the five sons of the king of the land of Judah..." are listed in these interesting and informative tablets. Beyond question Jehoiachin was the king, and dating according to his captivity, which commenced in the first year of his reign, would be expected.58

Turning from a specific discussion of dates to the general date of the book, we are supplied with excellent evidence by Otto Eissfeldt in his article entitled, "Das Datum der Belagerung von Tyros durch Nebukadnezar." For a long time two dates have been assigned to the thirteen year siege of Tyre: 598 to 585 B.C. and 585 to 572 B.C. The siege is attested in Josephus, and two references are made to it in Ezekiel's prophecy (26:1, 29:17). Josephus says that the siege began in the seventh year of Nebuchadrezzar (598 B.C.), whereas, according to Ezekiel, 586 B.C. would mark the beginning of the siege which was over before 570 B.C. (29:17).

Eissfeldt correctly assumes that Josephus was seeking to substantiate his Biblical dates for the destruction and restoration of Jerusalem as 585 B.C. and 537 B.C. respectively. By adding the reigns of various kings and judges who ruled over Tyre from the time of Ittobaal through the reign of one Eiromos a sum of fifty-four years and three months results. It is definitely stated that the siege of Tyre took place during the reign of Ittobaal. In the fourteenth regnal year of Eiromos Cyrus took power among the Persians. As we know, the reconstruction of the Temple began in the second year of Cyrus, which Josephus claims was fifty years after the city's destruction. This took place according to Phoenician reckoning in the fifteenth year of Eiromos of Tyre. By adding these figures to the date of the reconstruction we arrive at the date 586 B.C. as the time when the siege began; however, this does not fit in with the seventh year of Nebuchadrezzar.

As the Josephus text now stands, there is a strange, unexplainable grammatical peculiarity: the name, Nebuchadrezzar, appears in the genitive case as the subject of a sentence. Grammatical and factual difficulties quickly disappear by reading: ἑβδόμῳ μὲν γὰρ ἔτει τῆς Ἰωβάλου βασιλείας Ναβουχοδονοσωρ ἤρξατι πολιορκεῖν Τύρον.

"In the seventh year of the reign of Ittobaal began
Nebuchadrezzar to besiege Tyre."59

This reconstruction receives the support of Niese's Latin apparatus, where exactly the same explanation has been proposed. The dropping out of the name of Ittobaal would not be an unusual scribal mistake since numerous similar errors could be cited in ancient manuscripts. Just above this particular verse Josephus had been using Phoenician dates, hence we would naturally expect one here. Eissfeldt further shows that it would almost be inconceivable for Tyrians to date according to an outsider and not by their own king.

It was then during the reign of Ittobaal that Tyre was besieged for thirteen years. Beginning in the seventh year of his reign the siege ended thirteen years later with his overthrow in the twentieth year of his rule.[60]

This explanation of the Josephus date for the beginning of Nebuchadrezzar's siege of Tyre tends to establish the early sixth century B.C. as the date of Ezekiel. Ezekiel's historical allusions are proven to be absolutely correct; therefore, the book must belong between 593 and 570 B.C., as tradition has consistently maintained.[61]

A reconstruction of the Ideal Temple's East Gate found in Ez. 40:5ff. is further evidence indicating that Ezekiel lived before the Solomonic temple was destroyed. Only the East Gate is described in enough detail to allow for a relatively accurate reconstruction. By a careful comparison of the MT and the LXX we arrive at the following translation of the passage in question:

5. Behold a wall without the house round about and in the hand of the man a measuring rod of six cubits, by the cubit and span, and he measured the width of the structure one reed and (its) height one reed. 6. And he went into the gate which faces East and he went up seven steps and measured the vestibule of the gate, one reed wide. 7. The side chamber was one reed long and one reed wide and the pier between the side chambers five cubits and from the front of the vestibule of the gate from the house one reed. 8. And he measured the vestibule of the gate 9. eight cubits and its jambs two cubits. 10. And the side chambers of the East Gate were three on this side, and three on that side, all three with the same measurement, and all the jambs had one measurement. 11. And he measured the width of the gate's opening, ten cubits and the width thirteen cubits. 12. And the border before the side chambers one cubit on this side and one on that side and the side chamber was six cubits on this side and six cubits on that side. 13. And he measured the gate from the wall of the side

chamber to the wall of the side chamber, twenty-five
cubits wide opposite each other. 14. And he measured
the outer gate twenty cubits and the piers of the court
were six cubits. 15. And from before the front of the
gate without to the front of the vestibule of the gate
within, fifty cubits. 16. There were closed windows to
the side chambers within the gate and windows to the
vestibule within the gate roundabout and on the piers
were engaged pilasters.[62]

From this translation at least several aspects of the gate are
clear. There were three תאים which measured six cubits by
six cubits. That these were "side chambers" in a gate is con-
clusively shown by Von Soden's recent discovery of ta'u in Accadian literature with the same meaning.[63] Also we know that
there were at least two אילים (cf. Ugaritic 'alt, Gordon,
Ugaritic Handbook, p. 212) which measured five cubits by six
cubits plus a pair of smaller אילים measuring two cubits
length with an unknown width. By reading both the LXX and MT of
verse 14 we receive some light on two more אילים which were
by the court and measured 6 x 6 cu., thus accounting for the
earlier confusion of five cubits and six cubits in the LXX (see
Fig. 1).[64] We are told that the אלם of the gate was eight
cubits, but the אלם of the "gate toward the house" measured
six cubits or one reed (cf. vs.7). There must have been two
vestibules to the gate of varying depth. Our overall measurements for length are now as follows: outer אלם 8 cu., inner
אלם 6 cu., small אילים 2 cu., three תאים 18 cu., two
sets of אילים 10 cu. and one set of court אילים 6 cu.,
which adds up to the correct fifty cubits length. The gate
sockets were undoubtedly located behind the small piers which
served as jambs. By a composite reading of the LXX and MT we
were able to arrive at this clear picture of the overall length
of the gate.

As to the width of the gate, the overall measurement was
definitely twenty-five cubits from wall to wall. In the light
of our emended reading of verse 14 the outer vestibule was 20
cu. wide, and we may safely conclude that 13 cu. represents the
width of the " אלם toward the house." The actual opening of
the gate would then be 10 cu. as stated in the text. By a process of simple addition and subtraction we arrive at 1½ cu.
thickness for the walls at the back of the תאים. We thereby
have 6+6+10+3 = 25 cubits breadth (see Fig. 1).

This reconstruction is most probably correct in its main
outlines, but whether it represents a good picture of the gate
of a temple which once existed depends upon the accuracy of the
prophet's memory. The description is a reflection of a temple

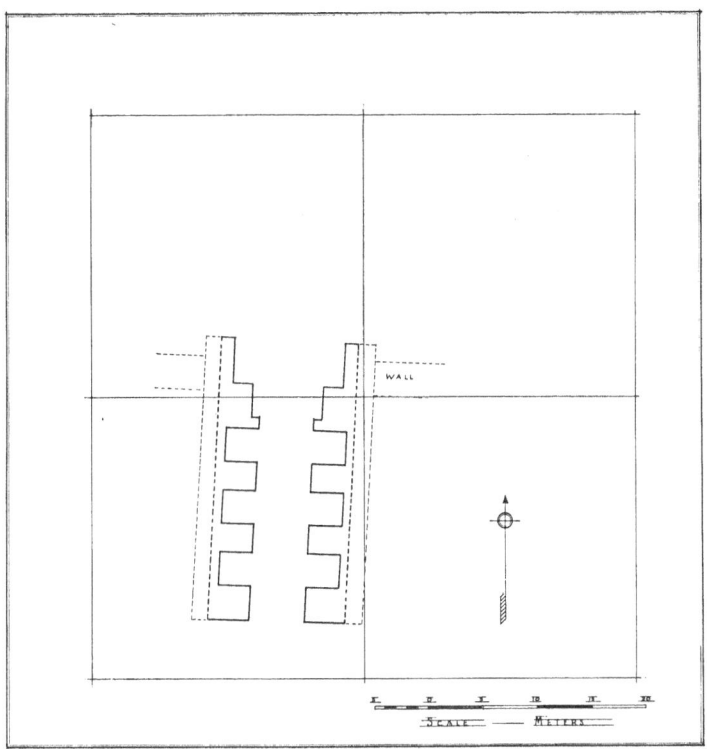

Fig. I. Suggested Plan of the East Gate.

structure quite familiar to the prophet. There is an amazing resemblance between this gate and the Solomonic gate at Megiddo, even to the extent that many of the measurements are almost identical (see Fig. 2).[65] Also there are definite affinities between the gate found here and Iron Age gates discovered at Carchemish.[66] Further comparison with the Solomonic gate excavated by Nelson Gleuck at Ezion-geber dates this type of construction in early preëxilic times, most probably during and immediately following Solomon's reign.[67] It is possible on the basis of the thickness of the walls of the gate of Megiddo (Fig. 2) that the corresponding walls in the East Gate should be thicker than $1\frac{1}{2}$ cubits (Fig. 1). However, our opinion is that the matter is relatively unimportant since the dimensions of the East Gate are visionary. Be that as it may, this type of gate disappeared from the ancient Near Eastern scene in the ninth century B.C., and Ezekiel must have seen the Solomonic gate of the Temple prior to the destruction of Jerusalem in 587

B.C. Stronger support for the traditional date of the book could hardly be asked. With this evidence the Torrey-Smith-Messel hypotheses must be finally and completely discarded. The date of Ezekiel should be placed between 593 and 570 B.C. since the major attacks on this position have failed and because positive evidence exists to support the traditional date.

Evidence such as that which Eissfeldt has presented in his fine article cannot be logically denied, nor can the presence of a Solomonic gate in the prophecy be overlooked. These two new facts provide the necessary foundation for the complete re-establishment of Ezekiel's date between 593 and 570 B.C.

Having shown therefore that Ezekiel's claims about date are correct, what can be said about the dates? Individual dates are correct, but not all the material between two given dates belongs there chronologically. The "thirtieth year," long a problem, proves to be a part of the regular dating scheme. Tradition and fact team up to certify that the date and dates of Ezekiel are correct.

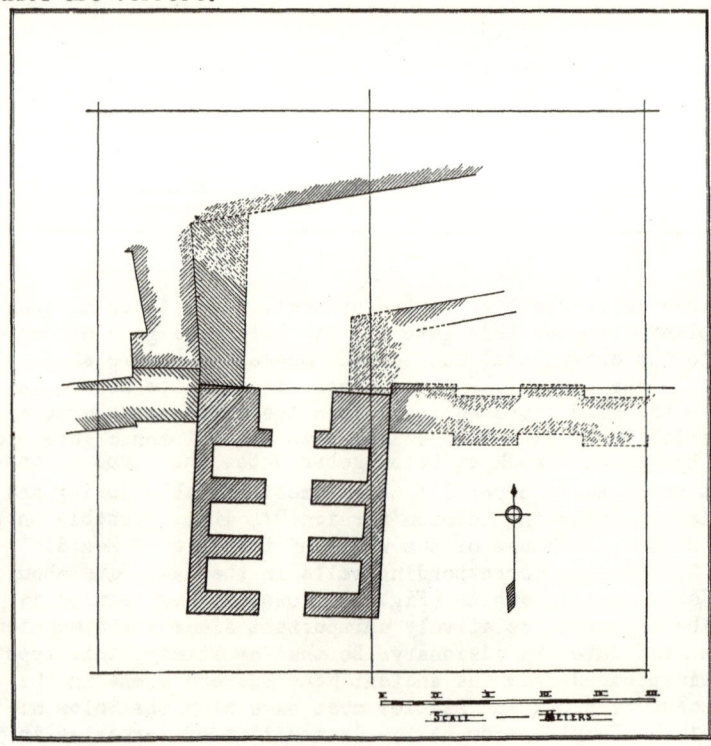

FIG. II. Solomonic Gate at Megiddo.

Chapter III

THE ARAMAIC IN THE BOOK OF EZEKIEL

A NEW STUDY of the Aramaic in Ezekiel has long been overdue, the last treatment having been made by Selle in 1890. In a doctoral dissertation on De Aramaismis libri Ezechielis he treated in detail Aramaic influence in the syntax, morphology and vocabulary of the book, that is, he discussed what was considered to be Aramaic.[1] Even though the flaws of this little work are not difficult to point out, still one must admit that it was a good study for its time. Granting that Selle made a good survey of the material does not, however, allow us or any other student of Ezekiel to accept his conclusions without restudy.

Lately Selle's monograph has received notice by C.C. Torrey and Shalom Spiegel, with each scholar lamenting the fact that this little book had so long been neglected. Neither Torrey nor Spiegel seems to have made an independent study of the material, and yet each draws diametrically opposite conclusions from Selle's discussion.[2]

Since 1890, needless to say, great progress has been made in our knowledge of Aramaic, its grammar and the history of its usage. Thanks to numerous Aramaic inscriptions and papyri which have been turned up since Selle's thesis our knowledge of the extent to which the language was used has greatly increased. We are therefore better equipped to recognise genuine Aramaic in the book and to use linguistic data as a criterion for dating the composition of the prophecy of Ezekiel.

The history of Arameans and Aramaic is long and difficult, but for an adequate understanding of the language we must briefly sketch their story. Although the beginnings of Aramean settlement in the Fertile Crescent go back into the second millennium, it is not the purpose of this chapter to discuss these elusive origins.[3] We shall take up their story with the foundation of Aram at Damascus. David had fought the Arameans on his borders and had defeated them; so complete was his victory that he captured Damascus and extended his empire elsewhere at their expense.[4] However, during the reign of Solomon a dynasty was established by Rezon at Damascus, which afterward became the political focal point of the Arameans.[5] This state was in constant contact with North Israel from the time of Solomon until the divided kingdom was absorbed into the Assyrian Empire. Sometimes the relations were peaceful with alliances being concluded and commerce being carried on; but more often there was bad blood between the two states.[6]

Though Aramaic inscriptions have been found which date as early as the ninth century B.C., our oldest inscription cannot be dated precisely. It was found at Tell Halaf and from epigraphical evidence is probably to be placed before any other inscription.[7] A votive stele of Ben-Hadad, found near Aleppo by M. Dunand and published in 1941, is, according to W.F. Albright, an inscription of Ben-Hadad I, which can easily be dated between 875 and 845 B.C. Such a date is proposed partly because this Ben-Hadad seems definitely to be the contemporary and bitter foe of Ahab, king of Israel.[8]

At Arslan Tash in the plain of Serug, east of Harran, F. Thureau Dangin and A. Barrois discovered three pieces of a line of Aramaic. Within this broken line is the name of לחזרא , Hazael, king of Damascus (cir. 840-800 B.C.). According to Thureau-Dangin and Barrois: "Le caractère paléographique de l'inscription justifie pleinement cette identification."[9]

The stele of Zakir, king of Hamath and Luʻash, is next in our chronological arrangement of early inscriptions, being dated around 775 B.C.[10] Finally the Zindjirli Aramaic inscriptions, including the stele of Panammu, are to be dated between about 775 and 725 B.C.[11] Our list of inscriptions is by no means complete, but those cited are sufficient to show the widespread use of Aramaic in the Fertile Crescent quite early in the first millennium B.C.[12]

As Bowman has pointed out, the political expansion of the Arameans was never co-extensive with their linguistic influence.[13] Assyria conquered many small and large Aramean states and incorporated them into her empire, but soon the conqueror began to use the language of the vanquished. This was true in part because the alphabetic Aramaic was much easier to use than the very complicated Assyrian cuneiform. As early as the time of Tiglath-pileser III records were kept in two languages: Assyrian and Aramaic. Reliefs coming from the time of Tiglath-pileser III and Sennacherib portray two scribes making records of the spoils from a captured city: one scribe has a stylus and a clay tablet, the other holds a quill and papyrus before him.[14] Assyrian records which were made in Aramaic have disappeared with the passage of time because of the material on which they were written, but the parallel records in Assyrian cuneiform are preserved on clay tablets. On these Assyrian tablets are found Aramaic dockets beginning during the reign of Tiglath-pileser III (745-727 B.C.) and becoming extremely numerous during the reign of Sennacherib and afterwards.[15] A docket usually consisted of one line which served as a filing reference for the keeper of the archives. Sometimes the Aramaic was added with quill and ink but just as often it was scratched in while the clay was still soft; thus indicating that professional scribes knew both Assyrian and Aramaic.[16] This also constitutes strong evidence that for many Assyrians Aramaic was already the normal language. These dockets are found down to the end of the Persian Empire, at which time Greek began to take the place of Aramaic as the lingua franca.[17]

Little triangular clay tablets began to appear by 674 B.C. and continue to be found until the fall of the Assyrian Empire (612 B.C.).[18] These small documents are business contracts in which the normal Assyrian script had given way completely to Aramaic cursive writing. Several such tablets from Assur, published by Lidzbarski, are to be dated after 659 B.C. and before 612 B.C.[19] Very probably the same dating should be given similar material unearthed at Tell Ḥalâf.[20] At any rate Aramaic was in extensive use as a commercial language during the seventh century B.C.

Not only had the language of the Arameans come into common usage in commerce, it also found its way into high political circles. Evidence of this fact is provided by the seal of "Pan-Assur, lord of the eunuchs of Sargon."[21] This seal impression was found at Khorsabad, the capital of the Assyrian Empire during Sargon's reign. Aramaic became more than a commercial language by the latter half of the eighth century B.C., when it was used as the international diplomatic language of the Near East. An incident during the siege of Jerusalem by Sennacherib in 701 B.C. is indicative of the place of this language in international relations. An Assyrian commander tried on this occasion to persuade the Jewish defenders of the city to give up the fight. In his propaganda effort Rab-shakeh spoke in Hebrew in order that the people might understand his plea. Immediately the royal officials, Eliakim, Shebna and Joab, requested that the Assyrian speak in Aramaic, which was well understood by them.[22] The official representatives of both Israel and Assyria probably negotiated in Aramaic, the normal diplomatic language, but the common people on the walls could not understand this international tongue. That Aramaic was the official language is further substantiated by the report of Beleṭir, a captain of the Assyrian cavalry. The report is written with ink in Aramaic script but with many "Assyrianisms."[23] Little doubt can remain that Aramaic had become the commercial and international language of the Assyrian world as early as the second half of the eighth century B.C.

Assyrian names for Jerusalem, Samaria and Judah in the eighth century B.C. reflect, not the Hebrew forms, but old Aramaic. **Ursalimmu** (pronounced **Uršalím**), the normal form for Jerusalem in Assyrian, is found in the Syriac ܐܘܪܫܠܡ and in the Nabatean אורשלם.24 Instead of Hebrew שֹׁמְרוֹן "Samaria," **Samerena** (pronounced **šāmerēn** with the regular Assyrian dialectal shift of sibilants) appears in Assyrian showing a phonetic position between Biblical Aramaic שָׁמְרַיִן (the old diphthongal pronunciation of classical Aramaic) and Syriac ܫܡܪܝܢ.25 The Biblical Aramaic form is a hypercorrection of the older Aramaic **Šāmerēn**, like Hebrew **Yerûšalaim** for older **Yerûšālēm**. Assyrian **Iaudu** (pronounced **Ya'ud**) is "Judah," so here again we have an old Aramaic form which is reflected by late Biblical Aramaic, **Yehûd**, which becomes **Ihûd** in Syriac. Not only the names of the capitals of the northern and southern kingdoms but the name Judah itself regularly appears in Assyrian inscriptions not in its Hebrew, but in an Aramaic form. We submit this as further evidence of the extensive use of this language in the Assyrian Empire.

When the Assyrian Empire was replaced by the Neo-Babylonian, Aramaic continued to hold its important place as an international tongue and greatly influenced the Neo-Babylonian language with which it co-existed. Aramaic dockets appear on Babylonian records as they had during Assyrian times. Actually the language of the Neo-Babylonian Empire was Aramaic; it was spoken in Mesopotamia in the seventh and sixth centuries B.C. and continued to be used very extensively in the Persian Empire.27 In the light of what has just been said the accuracy of Daniel 2:4, where Chaldeans speak to the king in Aramaic, is substantiated. This passage puzzled scholars for many years because Aramaic, they thought, could not possibly be the speech of the Chaldeans.28 The date of Daniel does not concern us here, but it is now certain that the writer followed correct tradition in making Aramaic the language of the Neo-Babylonians.

One of the most valuable Aramaic documents of the Neo-Babylonian period was found in a pottery jar at Saqqarah in 1942. A. Dupont-Sommer published it in 1948 and subsequently H.L. Ginsberg and John Bright discussed the document.29 It is a letter, to be dated a little earlier than the Lachish ostraca, which was sent by Adon, apparently king of Ashkelon, to the king of Egypt. Like Jehoiakim, Adon was facing the full fury of the Babylonian attack, and in his distress was seeking aid from the king of Egypt, whose vassal he was. Perhaps the king of Judah had sent similar Aramaic notes to the Egyptian court.30 Since this document is in Aramaic, we may safely conclude that it was the normal language used by Palestinians for diplomatic intercourse with the Egyptian court.

The above evidence is conclusive enough to establish the fact that Aramaic was the <u>lingua franca</u> of the Assyrian Empire. When the captives of Jerusalem arrived in Babylon (597 B.C.), they were confronted directly with the common usage of Aramaic. If Ezekiel, as tradition claims, was one of these exiles, perhaps some trace of Aramaic influence can be found in the work.

This chapter will take up the subject of the Aramaic influence in Ezekiel in the following manner: vocabulary, morphology and syntax. Selle's material will be discussed in exactly the same order as he presented it with the addition of more recent evidence. In order to simplify the task of discussing vocabulary it will be presented in glossary form. At the outset it should be stated clearly that not every mistake in the book is to be traced to Aramaic since Hebrew was also subject to scribal errors.

I. <u>Vocabulary</u>

1. בוץ (linen)- Ez. 27:16. This word, according to Selle, probably means "a very soft and precious kind of cloth" and is synonymous with שש, an Egyptian loan word, which is reflected in בוצא (Jast. p. 147) as well as قـ ﻣ (P. S. p. 39). Selle is not certain that it is an Aramaic loan word (Selle, pp. 40-41).[31] The same word, found in the Phoenician Kilamu Inscription (cir. 825 B.C.) and later in Accadian (būṣu), would appear to be a widely diffused trade term (later Greek <u>byssos</u>, which is used in the fifth century B.C.). The Edwin Smith Surgical Papyrus mentions "linen" used for bandaging, bdȝ, in four different passages. This dates from the late Middle Kingdom, that is to say, before 1500 B.C. and may well be the source of the word בוץ, according to Albright, since linen originally came from Egypt. The final weak laryngal was dropped early and would not appear in loan words.

2. בדק (breach) Ez. 27:9, 27 (for *batqu>badqu?). Selle would definitely take this to be Aramaic in origin (Selle p. 41). The Aramaic form is בדקא meaning "a breach, defect." This root, however, has now been found in an Amarna letter from Jerusalem (cir. 1375 B.C.). In Amarna 287, line 36, Albright reads <u>bat-qu-ú</u>, which he translates "breached."[32] The verb, <u>bataqu</u>, appears in Accadian with an identical meaning (B.G. p. 95).[33] In view of these facts its Aramaic origin is improbable.

3. ברק Ez. 1:14. Selle reads ברק with most scholars (Selle

p. 41). Since בקר is used in the previous verse and is found in the Targum and Vulgate, the problem is cleared up by this simple emendation.

4. בָּקַר (to inquire, seek after), Ez. 34:11, 12, is found in Lev. 13:36; 27:33, Ps. 27:4, Prov. 20:25, II Kgs. 16:15, and the same idea is met in the Targum and Syriac. It is thus a root common in preëxilic Hebrew as well as in Aramaic (cf. Selle, p. 41).

5. בָרַר (to cleanse, purge), Ez. 20:38, appears in what Selle calls "late writings," i.e., II Sam. 22:27 = Ps. 18:27, Zeph. 3:9, Job 33:3. The first passage, attested twice, is early preëxilic Hebrew, and the second is probably preëxilic also. Accadian barāru, "be or become bright, light," is an indication that ברר could easily have its source elsewhere than in Aramaic.

6. גָּדַף (to reproach, blaspheme) Ez. 20:27. To Selle this seems like an Aramaism, but it is also found in such clear preëxilic passages as Nu. 15:30, II Kgs. 19:6, 22, Is. 37:6, 23. Derivatives (גִּדּוּף and גְּדוּפָה) occur in Ez. 5:15; Is. 43:28; 51:7 and Zeph. 2:8. True, it appears in later Aramaic dialects but so do many very ancient Hebrew words. This root is very widespread, being found in Arabic, South Arabic and Ethiopic. Again it is necessary to contest Selle's dating of the above material and insist on this being a widely diffused Semitic root which is perfectly good Hebrew.

7. גַּלָּב (barber) Ez. 5:1. Used only here in the Bible, it becomes rather common in later Aramaic. However, the word is met in Accadian, gallābu, (M.A. p. 218),[34] from galābu, "to shave," and also occurs in Phoenician and Punic. This ancient root is continued in Syriac as ܓܠܒܐ, "a dagger or its sheath" and in Jewish Aramaic, גלב "to scrape, shave;" גַּלָּבָא "a barber." It is not Aramaic in origin but probably came into Hebrew through Phoenician or another Canaanite dialect.

8. גְּלוֹם (cloak) Ez. 27:24. Used in this one place but common in Aramaic, it is taken to be of Aramaic origin. However, the Aramaic is גְּלִימָא from which it would be very difficult to derive גְּלוֹם, yet the Accadian gelāmu (B.G. p. 98) would properly take the form found. The fact that the root גלם occurs in II Kgs. 2:8 further indicates a non-Aramaic source.

THE ARAMAIC IN THE BOOK OF EZEKIEL   53

9. גַּמָּדִים (?), Ez. 27:11, is said to mean "brave soldiers,"
   which meaning would square with the "brave soldiers of
   Tyre" (Selle p. 42). How Selle knew of this reputed bra-
   very of Tyrian soldiers is beyond our knowledge. גמדּ is
   possibly a mistake for גמר. a proposal which has often
   been made; note Ugaritic g͟m͟r͟m (Baal Epic). Syriac has ܓܡܪ
   "to finish, perfect" and ܓܡܝܪܐ "bold, daring, shameless"
   (P.S. p. 64). Explanation of form must remain in doubt at
   least for the time being.

10. דֹּחַן (millet), Ez. 4:2, is used in this one place, but
    דוֹחְנָיּא is common in Jewish Aramaic (cf. Jast. p. 284),
    and ܕܘܚܢܐ is found in Syriac (P.S. p. 85). There is
    strong likelihood that the word is either Aramaic or com-
    mon to both Aramaic and Hebrew of the time.

11. דָּיֵק (a watch tower) Ez. 4:2, 17:17, 21:27, 26:8, also Jer.
    52:4, II Kgs. 25:1. Undoubtedly דָּיֵק is an Aramaic ptc. of
    דוק, but the form is not normal (cf. קָיִם) and possibly
    indicates some archaic formation of the ptc. Also דָּיֵק is
    found only in passages where an Aramaic loan word could
    well be expected, and it is not known in Accadian. It con-
    stantly appears in later Hebrew and Aramaic, דוק, "to
    look with anxiety" (Jast. p. 288) and Syriac, ܕܘܩ, "to
    gaze, observe, look forth" (P.S. p. 87). Almost certainly
    דָּיֵק is Aramaic (cf. Hebrew הַמְחִיץ "the protecting thing,"
    ptc. formation).

12. דָּלִיָּת (branch) Ez. 17:6, 7, 23, 19:11, 31:1, 9, 12. In
    the late Hebrew of Rabbinical writings this word is often
    used, but in the Bible we meet it only in the above refer-
    ences and Jer. 11:16 (cf. דָּלִית Jast. p. 310). Since the
    word does not occur in Jewish Aramaic and appears in Arabic
    (dāliyah) as well as in Syriac, there is no good reason to
    assume Aramaic origin. Its occurrence in preëxilic Jeremi-
    ah suggests Hebrew.

13. דלח (to disturb, trouble), Ez. 22:2, 13, is not found
    elsewhere in the Bible but is fairly common in Assyrian,
    dalāḫu, "to disturb, disarrange" (M.A. p. 249). Of course,
    the word appears as דלח "to be anxious, fear" in Jewish
    Aramaic (Jast. p. 309) and in Syriac as ܕܠܚ "to trouble,
    discomfit" (P.S. p. 92); but it is probably an archaic
    root which carried over into later language. Needless to
    say, many very old words appear in kindred languages later
    without there being any borrowing one from the other.

14. דָּרוֹם (south) Ez. 21:2, 40:24, 27, 28, 44, 41:11, 42:12,

18, also Ec. 1:6, 11:3, Job 37:17, 14t, Dt. 33:23. Syriac does not use this, but it appears regularly in Christian Palestinian (G.B. p. 167)[35] referring to "South Palestine". The qātōl form (qātūl) indicates clearly that this Aramaic word was borrowed from Hebrew, not vice versa since the qāmeṣ in the Aramaic form does not represent original ā (cf. דְּרוֹמָיָא), but reflects Hebrew pretonic qāmeṣ.

15. זֹהַר (splendor) Ez. 8:12, also Dan. 12:13. It is entirely possible, even probable, that זהר had its origin in general Northwest Semitic since Ugaritic has the word zhr, "bright, pure (gem)" alternating with thr (= Hebrew טָהוֹר), and זהר may be derived indirectly from the former.[36] It is used in Aramaic, Arabic and Syriac with essentially the same meaning. The root is quite ancient but has been preserved in several Semitic languages.

16. זֶרֶת (span) Ez. 43:12 also Ex. 28:16, 39:9, Is. 40:12, I Sam. 17:4, cf. Syriac /ܙܪܬܐ/, "span" (P.S. p. 121). This word was originally borrowed in Northwest Semitic from Egyptian ḏrt, "hand span." This together with the fact that three of the four passages where it occurs are preëxilic makes it safe to conclude that the word is good Hebrew.

17. חֲבֹל; חֲבֹלָה (a pledge) Ez. 18:7, 12, 16, 33:15 also Dan. 3:25, 6:24, Ezra 4:22. In Amos 2:8 the root חבל occurs with regard to "clothing taken in pledge," and is also met in Prov. 13:13, 20:16, 27:13, Ex. 22:25, Dt. 24:6, Zech. 11:7, 14, Ct. 8:5. The Accadian verb habālu "to pledge, promise" and the noun hubullu, "interest, guarantee, pledge" (M.A. p. 301) are further proof that this is not a "late" word. Syriac has ܚܒܠ "to twist, writhe in pain" (P.S. p. 123), and Jewish Aramaic retains חבל, "to seize, to take a pledge" (Jast. p. 420). A Hebrew word of possible Accadian origin has passed into the later dialects with real changes of meaning.

18. חסם Ez. 39:11 (to shut up, restrain) also Dt. 25:4 "to muzzle the ox" and Ps. 39:2 "let me keep a muzzle for my mouth." Jewish Aramaic has חֲסַם "to muzzle, restrain, silence" (Jast. p. 488) with cognates in Accadian and Arabic. In the light of its occurrences חסם is an old Hebrew word and hence was borrowed from Hebrew by Jewish Aramaic.

19. טרף (a leaf) Ez. 17:9. With the meaning "leaf" טַרְפָּא is frequently used in Aramaic. Since the context here requires such a meaning, we may safely admit that while this

root often occurs in Hebrew with the meaning "tear, rend," the word meaning "leaf" is almost certainly Aramaic.

20. כָּהָה (to be disheartened) Ez. 13:2. Selle states categorically that this is to be equated with the Syriac verb ܟܗܐ; and since it is found only in late passages (i.e., Dan. 11:30, Ps. 109:16, Job 30:9), it is to be considered Aramaic (Selle, p. 43). The reader should be reminded that the Hebrew root כהה (Gn. 27:1, Dt. 34:7, Is. 42:4, Zech. 12:17, Job 17:7, Ez. 21:12) has the same meaning and that כאה may just as well be an Aramaic spelling reflecting an Aramaized form of this root.

21. כָּחַל (to paint) Ez. 23:40. Undoubtedly the meaning arose from the stibium which women used for eye paint. Here alone the root, כחל, appears but its equivalent, פוך, is a more extensively used Hebrew word. When Sennacherib was counting his spoil at Jerusalem, mention was made of gu-uḫ-li "stibium," which must have been a common trade term.[37] Possibly it came from Aramaic commercial terminology, but terms such as these fast become "international words." The fact that this is the only occurrence of a word derived from this root in Hebrew and that the common Hebrew term is פוך makes the assumption that this is a loan word plausible.

22. כָּפֵן (to become languid) Ez. 17:7. In Job 5:22, 30:3 כָּפֵן means "famine," but the root is not found elsewhere in the Old Testament. Cf. Jewish Aramaic כפן "to be hungry, to starve" (Jast. p. 660) and Syriac ܟܦܢ "to hunger." Since the word is so rare in Hebrew and is used only in books of relatively late composition, the evidence points strongly to Aramaic origin.

23. לִשְׁכָּה (room) is found many times in Ezekiel, but it is also used so widely in Hebrew that an Aramaic origin, Selle admits, could not be substantiated. The fact that it appears in I Sam. 9:22, II Kgs. 23:11 et al makes it certain that this common Hebrew word is not Aramaic in origin.

24. מגר (to throw, toss Ez. 21:17, Ps. 89:45, Ezra 6:12. A common word in Jewish Aramaic, מְגַר "to drag down, to throw over" (Jast. p. 730), it is rather rare in Biblical Hebrew, but there is no good reason to consider it a late addition to the Hebrew vocabulary since the occurrence in Ps. 89 is definitely early.

25. מַדְרֵגָה (steep place) Ez. 38:20 and Ct. 2:14. Confidently

Selle traces the root of this word to Aramaic, דַּרְגָּא "a step, stair, degree," but quick acceptance of this equivalence would be dangerous since Accadian has <u>dargu</u>, "pathway in mountainous region" (B.G. p. 109; M.A. p. 268). This root is found in Arabic, Jewish Aramaic, Syriac and Accadian. Since the form is characteristically Hebrew, the infrequent appearance of the root in the Bible does not militate against its being Hebrew. It is well to remember that the vocabulary of the Hebrew Bible is far from being a complete vocabulary of Biblical Hebrew.38

26. מִשְׁטַח; מִשְׁטוֹח (net Ez. 26:5, 14, 47:14. Occurring only here, its presence is, according to Selle, the work of an "Aramaic interpreter" (Selle p. 43). True, these forms are unique, but the root appears in Nu. 11:32, II Sam. 17:19, Is. 8:2, Job 12:23 and Ps. 88:10. and the form mištōaḥ (mištāḥ) is characteristically Hebrew. Admittedly the root finds wider usage in later Aramaic (Jast. p. 1553), yet the presence of a strictly Hebrew form in the above passages points definitely to Hebrew origin.

27. סָגָן (prefect, ruler) Ez. 23:6, 12, 23. Clearly a political term such as this had its origin with the Accadian šaknu, "governor" (later pronounced <u>sagan</u>) from <u>šakānu</u>, "to put, place, appoint." It would be expected that the Assyrian word for an official would quickly find its way into the languages of all vassal peoples. It becomes common in late Hebrew (e.g., Jer. 51:23, 28, 57, Ezra 9:2, Neh. 2:16 <u>et al</u>). This word comes undoubtedly from Aramaic, which was the <u>lingua franca</u> of the Assyrian Empire as early as the eighth century B.C. (cf. above).

28. סִלּוֹן (thorn) Ez. 2:6, 28:24. The etymology of this word is unknown. It occurs only twice in the Bible but is met often as סִלּוָא in later Hebrew (Jast. p. 993) and Syriac (P.S. p. 378). No conclusion about its origin is possible at this juncture.

29. סָרָב for sarrāb (rebellious) Ez. 2:6, is not found elsewhere. Jewish Aramaic has סְרָב "to decline, refuse" (Jast. p. 1021) while Syriac uses ܣܪܒ "to prate, to boast" (P.S. p. 389). Scholars generally have taken it to be an Aramaic loan word (B.D.B. p. 709, G.B. p. 552). While it is admitted that our evidence is not conclusive, the word is probably Aramaic. However, the form is just as good in Hebrew as in Aramaic.

30. עֲזָרָה (an enclosure) Ez. 43:14 also II Chr. 4:6, 9, 12.

THE ARAMAIC IN THE BOOK OF EZEKIEL   57

This word is found more frequently in late Hebrew (Jast. p. 1062) and is also used in Jewish Aramaic, עֲזָרְךָ "temple forecourt." It appears in Syriac, ܥܪܐ meaning "to entangle, enclose" (P.S. p. 409). Late and scant usage in the Bible plus a later development in Aramaic and Syriac indicate a probable Aramaic origin.

31. עָמַם (to conceal, hide) Ez. 28:3, 31:8 also Lam. 4:1, cf. עָמַם "to be dim, to quench, press," (Jast. p. 1089). This rare Biblical word is common in Aramaic, which probably means it came into Hebrew *via* Aramaic.

32. עֲרוּגָה (terrace, bed) Ez. 17:4, 10, Ct. 5:13. There is no Aramaic equivalent for this Hebrew word nor does it occur in Syriac; however, the stem is found in several Semitic languages. It may represent a late addition to Hebrew vocabulary, but we hardly think its source was Aramaic since the word is conspicuously absent from Aramaic dialects.

33. עֲרִיסָה (dough) Ez. 44:30 also Nu. 15:20, 21; Neh. 10:38. No Aramaic equivalent is known. This plus the fact that the references in Numbers are old leads us to conclude that the form is good preëxilic Hebrew.

34. פֶּחָה (governor, leader) Ez. 23:6, 12, 23. This name for a political official is quite common in Hebrew (cf. I Kgs. 20:24, II Kgs. 18:14 = Is. 36:9, Jer. 51:28, 57 et al) and in Biblical Aramaic (cf. Ezra 5:3, 6, 14, 6:6, 7, 13; Dan. 3:2, 3, 27, 6:1). Assyrian has paḫātu (originally bēl-piḫāti) "prefect or prefecture" (M.A. pp. 797-799) from which it became an international Aramaic word. Like סְגָן (cf. above) this is an official title which Assyrian conquerors introduced and which continued among their vassals. The form is distinctly Hebrew, hence it is possible that Biblical Aramaic borrowed it from Hebrew.

35. פַּנַּג (millet) Ez. 27:17. There is but this one occurrence in the Bible, and the meaning is somewhat uncertain. Conceivably the Syriac ܦܢܓܐ, "a kind of millet," is the same word, but Selle is wrong in deriving it from פתה "to be enticed" (Selle p. 44). A more logical approach through Accadian gives pannigu, from seventh century B.C. texts of Assurbanapli which reflect earlier sources.[39] The meaning remains a question, as does the origin.

36. פרח (to fly) Ez. 13:20. Selle maintains that the normal Hebrew meaning, "to flower, germinate," is absent in this

case, therefore he thinks that the common Aramaic verb פרח "to fly" should be read. It is important to note that the primary meaning of this Aramaic term is "to bloom" with the secondary meaning "to fly" (Jast. p. 1223). The latter meaning appears very often in Aramaic and Syriac (P.S. p. 458) but occurs in Hebrew only in this passage, hence the root in this meaning is probably borrowed from Aramaic.

37. פָּכָה (to trickle, drip) Ez. 47:2. This particular form occurs but once in the Bible: פַּךְ, "vial, flask for anointing" appears in I Sam. 10:1, II Kgs. 9:1, 3 which carries over into later Hebrew with the same meaning (Jast. pp. 1173-4). This is of Hebrew origin.

38. פַּתוֹת (morsel) Ez. 13:19. Selle fails to list all the occurrences of this word and so leads the casual reader to the erroneous conclusion that it is very rare (Selle p.45). A list of the appearances of this word in the Bible points strongly to a Hebrew origin (cf. Gen. 18:5, Ju. 19:5, I Sam. 2:36, 28:22, I Kgs. 17:11 et al. The word is not Aramaic in origin.).

39. צוּרָה (form, fashion) Ez. 43:11. This form is found only here, but the verb צוּר, "to fashion, delineate," occurs in Ex. 32:4, I Kgs. 7:15, Jer. 1:15. Both verb and noun are continued in Jewish Aramaic and Syriac (P.S. p. 476); however, the word came originally from Accadian uṣurtu, whence ṣurtu, as Zimmern has pointed out. The verbal forms usually derived from צוּר probably came from יצר, and צוּרָה is probably Aramaic. The fact that ṣurtu does occur in Accadian shows beyond reasonable doubt that Aramaic ṣurtâ is derived therefrom (cf. Bruno Meissner, Studien Zur assyrischen Lexikographie, III, pp. 57-58). It is very probable that the word came into Aramaic and Hebrew from Accadian at about the same time.

40. צְפִירָה (doom) Ez. 7:7, 10, Is. 28:5. The exact meaning in Ezekiel is obscure, since "crown" seems to fit very badly, but "doom" is a possible solution on the basis of Accadian ṣapāru "to destroy" (M.A. p. 886). However, such a meaning does not occur in Jewish Aramaic, where צְפִירָא "a circle, crown" (Jast. p. 1297) is met. "Doom" fits much better and perhaps indicates a non-Aramaic source.

41. צרב (to be consumed) Ez. 21:3. This word, which appears only once in the Bible, is to be related to Accadian ṣarābu, "to burn, to scorch." In Jewish Aramaic צָרְבָא,

THE ARAMAIC IN THE BOOK OF EZEKIEL   59

"shrinking, reduction through smelting," (Jast. p. 1299) must be cognate with the earlier Assyrian verb since they both are connected in meaning with the action of fire. Here we probably have a borrowing from Accadian on the part of both Hebrew and Aramaic. It is, however, possible that the Hebrew word came via Aramaic.

42. קהה (to be blunt, dull) Ez. 18:2, Jer. 31:29, 30, Ec. 10: 10. Selle is certain that the verb comes from Aramaic קהא and Syriac ܩܗܐ "to be dull, blunt" (Selle p. 45). The lateness of the word must be called in question on the basis of קהיון in Amos 4:6, where one would hardly expect to meet Aramaic. There is no reason to think that the word was not common to both Hebrew and Aramaic.

43. קנין (acquisition) Ez. 38:12, 13ff. and Gen. 34:23, Prov. 4:7. Although usage of this unusual form is rare, the root appears rather widely in other Hebrew forms (cf. Gen. 31:18, 36:6, Jos. 14:4 et al). We have qny in Ugaritic, and it is met in Phoenician.[40] This is a Hebrew word of early origin; and though the -ân ending is possibly Aramaic in vocalization, the consonantal base qnyn is certainly good early Hebrew.

44. קטף (to pluck, to cut) Ez. 17:4, 22 also Dt. 23:26, Job 30:4, 8:2. This word is obviously common to Hebrew and Aramaic; it also appears in Accadian and as a very early loan word from Canaanite in Egyptian (Eg. qdf, i.e. qtf, appears first in the Middle Kingdom about 1800 B.C. or earlier).

45. קסת (palette) Ez. 9:2. Selle assumes that this noun, met once in the Bible, is to be derived from the proposed Hebrew root קשה "to be covered" because the small vessel of the scribe (i.e., ink well) was generally covered (Selle p. 46). The noun, according to Selle, corresponds to Jewish Aramaic קסתה "a flat dish, vessel for libation" and has its formal origin there. However, he is entirely wrong. The Egyptian gsty, "scribal palette," gives us the exact origin of the word.[41] Egyptian g was reproduced by q in Hebrew.[42] In any case the word is not Aramaic.

46. קפדה (fearfulness, trembling) Ez. 7:25, Is. 38:12. The form קפד "hedgehog" is found in Is. 14:23, 34:11 and Zech. 2:14. The word is probably good Hebrew.

47. רסס (to dampen, moisten) Ez. 46:14. Except for רסיס "drop," Ct. 5:2, this is the only appearance of the root

in Hebrew, but רְסִיסִים "raindrop" is met often in Jewish
Aramaic. Some sort of Aramaic influence may readily be admitted, but its exact nature escapes us.

48. רָצֹא(?) Ez. 1:14. LXX omits the entire verse, which
looks very much like an interpolation. The Vulgate reads
יָצֹא. The whole verse is questionable, and רצוא looks
like a mistake. We doubt that רצוא is to be taken as the
Aramaic form of רוץ, for we would expect an altered root
in that language by regular phonetic change.

49. שַׁלִּיט (from שלט "to dominate, to be master of") Ez. 16:30
also Gen. 42:6, Ec. 8:8. The root is used in practically
every language of the ancient Near East, cf. Accadian
šalāṭu, Jewish Aramaic שלט(Jast. p. 1583), Syriac, Arabic,
etc. In Ugaritic it appears in the secondary noun šlyt,
with consonantal yodh (cf. Gordon pp. 272-274). This is an
old Hebrew root, and the form is not necessarily Aramaic
(cf. צַדִּיק).

50. שַׁלְהֶבֶת(flame) Ez. 21:3, Job 15:30, Ct. 8:6. Generally
this has been traced to a shaphel formation of the noun,
which was supposed to indicate a late date since ܫܠܗܒ is
a common stem. Of course, להב is an old root, hence we are
concerned here with the age of shaphel formations. Shaphel
formations occur not only in Assyrian but in Ugaritic and
other Northwest Semitic dialects.[43] As a matter of fact,
the shaphel and hištaphel are the normal forms for express-
ing the causative in Ugaritic. Thanks to Ugaritic we now
recognise in the form הִשְׁתַּחֲוָה a hištaphel form from the
חוי(cf. Gordon p. 228). One would expect that some of
these forms from neighboring languages would find their
way into the everyday speech of the Hebrews. The shaphel
form could well indicate not an Aramaic origin but a very
early Northwest Semitic source for the above form.

51. שָׁרוֹת (?) Ez. 27:25. The problem of how to translate
שרות has puzzled scholars for a long time. A simple emendation on the basis of Is. 2:16b makes a sensible rendering possible. We read שְׂכִיּוֹת by changing ר to כ and re-
storing the yodh, which probably dropped out in transmission. Albright, in his forthcoming article on "Baal-Zephon"
for the Bertholet Festschrift, shows that skt means "ship"
in Ugaritic and points out the rather common skt(y) in E-
gyptian with the same meaning. A remarkable parallel between Isaiah and Ezekiel can easily be seen. They appear
as follows: אניות הרשיש שכיותיך מערב Ez. 27:25 e-
mended.   ועל כל-אניות תרשיש ועל כל-שכיות החמדה Is. 2:

16b. Since "the ships of Tarshish" are then parallel to
שכיות in Ezekiel as well as in Isaiah, we can safely
make the emendation which shows that the origin of the
word goes far back beyond the period of Aramaic influence.
The passage is to be translated "ships of Tarshish, thy
ships of merchandise."

52. תָּפֵל (marly clay plaster) Ez. 13:10, 11, 14, 15; 22:28
and Job 6:6. This word is found only in late Biblical
books, becoming fairly common in later Hebrew תָּפֵל "to
paste." The word is not found in Aramaic or Syriac, hence
its source must be sought somewhere else.

After close examination of the so-called Aramaic words in
Ezekiel we find only nine of them which can certainly be connected with Aramaic. Among these nine are סבן and פחה, which
were a part of the seventh century B.C. Aramaic lingua franca
of the Near East. Nine more words may possibly be related to
Aramaic roots or forms. Two words are beyond explanation. Finally, at least thirty-two of the fifty-two words discussed
have no connection whatever with Aramaic. We can safely say,
therefore, that Aramaic influence in Ezekiel's vocabulary was
slight indeed.

II. Morphology

Not only does the vocabulary of Ezekiel's book reflect this
slight influence, Aramaisms are even more evident in the morphology of this prophetic work. Again we follow the order taken
by Selle in discussing the material involved.

First we shall deal with certain examples of regular phonetic change between Hebrew and Aramaic in Ezekiel. Selle is correct in deriving קוּם (Ez. 6:9; 20:43; 36:31) from קיץ, seeing
the change as regular shift of צ to ס. The Aramaic סטנה appears
for the Hebrew העגה in Ez. 13:10. חד (33:10) is the result of
Aramaic influence as is the introduction of ר in סרגפה (31:5).
All these are rather definite Aramaisms, but Selle refers to
others which are not so certain (cf. Selle pp. 14-16).

Two distinct roots are represented by שד (23:3, 8, 21) and
דד (Aramaic, according to Selle) which do not reflect a normal
phonetic change. Selle's analogy with די and הד does not hold
because there is no regular interchange of ש and ד (Selle p.14).

A rather difficult problem is the interchange of על and אל
which Selle sees as the result of Aramaic influence (Selle p.
14). The change is due to confusion between the prepositions at
the hand of later transcribers when the force of א had been

lost. Basis for such a conclusion is: (a) על and אל are interchanged in the same verse (cf. Ez. 21:12, 44:13, Is. 22:15, Jer. 18:11 et al); (b)interchange is found in parallel passages in different books (e.g., II Sam. 6:10 = I Ch. 13:13; I Kgs. 22:6 = II Ch. 18:15 et al). Sometimes this is true even in the same book, e.g., Ez. 1:12 = 1:20.[44]

Selle believes that אלמנותיו (Ez. 19:7; 22:25) should be read ארמנותיו which the context seems to require, and so he thinks it is an Aramaic change of ל to ר. There is no such regular change in Aramaic; and since the form with "l" appears also earlier, it seems that an *almôn coexisted with armôn "gate tower;" (see Koehler-Baumgartner p. 88b). For this view there is some extra-Hebrew evidence; cf. the Accadian variants Arman, Alman, Halman for Aleppo and homonymous place names meaning originally something like "citadel" (W.F. Albright).

The place name כנה (27:23) is not a shortened form of כלנה (Gn. 10:10), as Selle presumed, where the ל has assimilated to the נ (cf. Selle p. 15). Kannu' is to be located somewhere in Assyria and has no connection with Calneh.[45] In any case, there is no reason to consider כנה an Aramaic form.

Again Selle is incorrect in seeing Aramaic influence in what seems to be the loss of intervocalic ה in the form וני (< וְהָנִי), "wail," 27:32 (cf. Selle p. 16). Such syncope is met in both Hebrew and Aramaic, and a conclusion that this is the result of Aramaic influence is not justified. Selle assumes that למשעי (Ez. 16:4) corresponds to an Aramaic construct of a noun in -ît, t being regularly lost in Aramaic constructs of nouns -ût, ît. His assumption may be correct (Selle p. 16). In הזֹ (40:45) Selle sees an inclination toward Aramaic, but the form is simply a by-form of Hebrew זאת (<zât) without -t and with different spelling for final ô (e.g. אתנה).

The form of פארת (Ez. 17:6, 31:5, 8, 12, 13) is said by Selle (p. 17) to be an example of the loss of an intervocalic א which he considers an Aramaic process. There is no evidence that the form is not good Hebrew; א also quiesced in Hebrew.

There are certain unusual independent pronominal forms which Selle considers Aramaic. אַתְּ (28:14) appears as a masculine form, which Selle (p. 19ff.) considers Aramaic. The same form is used however in Nu. 11:15, Dt. 5:24. In the passage in Ez. Greek and Syriac both read אַתְּ, hardly a correct rendering. It may be an Aramaized form (cf. Bib. Aram. אַנְתְּ).

The final n of masc. אתן (34:31) may be due to Aramaic in-

THE ARAMAIC IN THE BOOK OF EZEKIEL   63

fluence (cf. Bib. Aram. יָעֲטִין, Syriac ܥܛܐ, ܛܐ) though
Selle explains it as a slip of the pen. Another apparent mixing
of genders is seen in 13:20, where עֲשֶׂיתֶן is used in a feminine
sense. Very probably this is to be explained as vertical or
horizontal dittography. In the line above יְהֹוָה is read, and just
after the pronoun אֲנִי is found. Either word could have brought
about a ת- for נ-mistake. At any rate the form is not an Aramaism
as Selle asserts (Selle p. 19). In all these passages the unusual forms may be due to errors of the copyist.

An תָ- ending of the verb, instead of הָ (cf. 24:12, 46:17),
could be either an archaic form, a late form or possibly the
scribal error of one who knew Aramaic. For עָשִׂית (16:159) Selle
(p. 21) reads עֲשִׂית , considering it apparently as an Aramaic
first person perfect form like Syriac ܥܒܕܬ . The form is probably merely a defective spelling of the Hebrew first person
singular. There is no reason to consider אַתְּי (Qere: 'att),
which is met frequently in chapter 16, as an Aramaism; we face
nothing more than a historical spelling of an old form of the
feminine pronoun. The yodh is actually read in Ju. 17:2, I Kgs.
4:16, 23; 8:1, etc. and is very commonly found in the new Isaiah Scroll.

Selle (p. 21) considers the suffix הֶן (33:26), used where
one would naturally expect הֶם, an Aramaism. He concludes that
the prophet in speaking to audiences composed of both sexes
used both genders interchangeably as suffixes (Selle p. 21).
Biblical Aramaic has suffix (masc.) plural הוֹן , but Elephan-
tine has הֶן (A. Cowley, *Aramaic Papyri*, p. 26). An Aramaic-
using copyist evidently used the current Aramaic spelling, inadvertently following correct הֶם in the same passage.

Again a mixing of genders is evident in הִקָּרְבוּ (37:7), where
the 2 m. pl. has replaced the 3 f. pl. (the Aramaic form would
be yiqrĕbān). Many emendations have been suggested, such as
יִקְרְבוּ or הִקָּרַבְנָה , but our problem is the text as it stands.
Most probably this is the result of a scribal mixing of genders
at an early date in the course of textual transmission, when
Aramaic-using scribes were unfamiliar with Hebrew grammar.

Our attention now turns to verbal forms which seem to bear
the imprint of Aramaic influence. Undoubtedly one of the most
difficult forms is the ptc. הַיֹּשְׁבָתִי . Whence the final י?
Perhaps it is a carry-over from an old genitive ending. The
same sort of form occurs in Jer. 10:17, 22:23, Lam. 4:20, and
it is read in Gen. 49:11, Is. 22:16, Mic. 7:14, etc., as well
as this case in Ez. 27:3. We do not know what to make of it.

Selle noticed that the infinitives with feminine terminations in Ez. 16:5 לְחֻמְלָה, 21:16 לְמָרְטָה, 22:3 לְשָׁמְעָה, 44:25 לְשָׁמְעָה, closely resemble the infinitive formations in the derived conjugations of Aramaic. These forms are not Aramaic; they are nothing more than Hebrew infinitives with feminine terminations.

The pa‛el inf. form of Aramaic seems definitely to underly the nouns קְלָקָה (22:4), גְּעָצָה (35:12) and בַּלָּהוֹת (26:21, 27:36, 28:19). The case of כְּבַקָּרַת (34:12) is more involved since it probably is a result of dittography and was not originally an Aramaic formation at all. It should be read כְּבַקֵּר. Such a mistake might easily have come about in the following way. The form immediately preceding כבקרת is וּבִקַּרְתִּים. Any scribe could have been guilty of the dittography of the letters בקרת. Plainly מִגְרָשָׁה is the pa‛el infinitive with a prefixed מ, a definite Aramaic influence. An Aramaizing infinitive of נשא is seen in לְמַשְׂאוֹת (17:9) and not, as Selle thinks, a form of משא, where ל"ה and ל"א have been mixed.

A scribal mistake accounts for יִדְרְשׁ (14:3) where we should find הִדָּרֵשׁ, a niphal infinitive which is probably good Hebrew. In the case of מֵהֲקָצְצוֹת (46:12) the ה has not been lost as is the normal process in Hebrew. The failure of an intervocalic ה to drop out is more common to Aramaic than to Hebrew.

Unusual verbal formations are generally explained by Selle as Aramaisms. However, נִפְלִי (28:23) is correctly attributed by him to a slip of the pen for נפל. More difficult to explain is שאשׁ from אאשׁ or שוא. It is a pilpel formation, but such forms are found in Is. 14:23, 17:11, 22:5, Nu. 24:17, Jer. 48:45. Admittedly these unusual verb formations become more common in Aramaic, but they do not necessarily point to an Aramaic origin. An incorrect vocalization accounts for וְנִסָּדוּ (23:48) which should be simply וְנוֹסְדָה, an ordinary niphal form.

A study of certain weak verbs reveals a few rare forms. In לְהַנִּיחַ (22:20) the ה of the hiphil in this intervocalic position is not syncopated, but that does not necessarily indicate Aramaic influence (cf. לְהַקְטִיל). עָחֵל (39:7) is probably an Aramaized form of the hiphil as Selle maintains (Selle p. 27).⁴⁶

The פ"א verbs reveal the weakening of the א which quiesces, changes to י or disappears in Ez. (cf. 42:5, יוֹכְלוּ; 21:33, לְהָכִיל). Both Hebrew and Aramaic have weakened alephs, hence we are unable to detect Aramaic morphology here.

The verb שאט (16:57 הַשָּׁאטוֹת, 25:6 שָׁאטְךָ, 15 בִּשְׁאָט 36:5

THE ARAMAIC IN THE BOOK OF EZEKIEL

בְּשָׂאוֹ) is an י"ו verb with a mediae א' inserted, which is a true Aramaism, according to Selle (Selle p. 28). The use of לָאט (Ju. 4:21) for לוט and קָהַם (Hosea 10:14) for קום makes one doubt whether he is correct.

Aramaic is clearly seen in the infinitive form קְנֹה (Ez. 13:6) found elsewhere only in late passages (cf. Ruth 4:7, Esther 9:29, 31, 32). The mixture of ה"ל and א"ל verbs is cited by Selle as an indication of Aramaic influence. Such mixing also took place in Hebrew, but the extensive mixing possibly points to the hand of an Aramaic scribe (cf. Selle p. 29).

A strange infinitive absolute form הָחֵה (21:15) is a puzzle, but actually some sort of mistake may account for the form which is better read חָיֹה. Finally, among verb forms Selle cites וְנֶעֱנוּ לוֹ (36:3) which perhaps appears to be halfway between <u>qal</u> and <u>niphal</u> forms, but the exact explanation is unknown to us.

The noun has not completely escaped Aramaic influence, but the extent of that influence is indeed scant. Two forms, פְּקַב (13:9) and יָקָר (1:20), are unquestionably Aramaic. Twice we meet the plural ending יִ֯ן- instead of Hebrew ים- (cf. 4:9, 28:18), and in at least two cases feminine endings exhibit Aramaic orthography (cf. קִדְמָא 27:31, לִבְנָא 19:2). Above reference has been made to pa'el formations of several nouns, possibly another mark of Aramaic.

Regarding בְּקָרָתָה (28:13) Selle is correct in calling the ending an old Semitic form, not a late Aramaic introduction (Selle p. 33). בָּלָא (36:5) represents an exchange of <u>mater lectionis</u> א for ה which would be a mistake to be expected from an Aramaic scribe. As a matter of fact, the variant reading has the regular Hebrew spelling with final ה.

Though endings ני- and נה- have often been taken as signs of late linguistic development, the נה- ending is very old. As early as the fifteenth century B.C. a prince of Taanach used specifically the Canaanite word <u>ha-at-nu-tam</u>, "betrothal."[47] Usage of these two endings most assuredly is more frequent in later language, but to say that they are the product of a later time is going much too far.

Finally, the noun אַתִּיקֶהָא (41:15) presents a riddle. Seemingly we have an Aramaic suffix הא instead of regular הָ, as found earlier in the same section. Obviously some Aramaic-using scribe in the course of textual transmission inadvertently added an א.

The failure of the article to be syncopated under regular conditions, according to Selle, definitely reveals an Aramaic tendency to treat ה in this way; but since there is no prepositive article in Aramaic, it cannot well be considered an Aramaism. Two examples present themselves: פְּתֻחֹת לוֹת (40:25) and לַהֲגָרִים (47:22).

Other words of interest include בֵּיה used instead of the preposition בֵּין twice (cf. 1:27; 41:9); however, in both cases the LXX deletes what is probably a late interpolation. Ewald maintained that קְבָל (26:9) is the Aramaic preposition (cf. Selle p. 34), but closer examination of the passage is necessary to understand our contrary conclusion. The MT reads קָבֳלּוֹ וּמְחִי. Assyrian qablu = "battle" suggests that the word may have something to do with a "siege engine" of some kind. There was a Hebrew מחה "to strike" (Nu. 34:11), giving us a suitable translation, "and the blow of his siege engine."[48] The interjection הֵא is very probably Aramaic (cf. Bib. Aram. הָא), but its use in Gen. 47:23 makes one wonder if it were not common to Aramaic and Hebrew.

Aramaic morphology has apparently had a small but in some respects an important influence on the text of Ezekiel. Verb forms, noun endings and pronominal alterations head the list of Aramaisms in the morphological makeup of the book. This influence is, as one would expect, far stronger than the Aramaic loan words in vocabulary since an Aramaic-using scribe would be far more likely to make a formal mistake than to change a word from Hebrew to Aramaic.

III. Syntax

Evidence of Aramaic syntax is very difficult to find in the book of Ezekiel. Twice ל is used as a sign of the indirect object (26:3, 37:11), which possibly indicates Aramaic influence. Whether הִנְנִי אֲנִי (6:3) is a sign of later linguistic development is also open to question since similar constructions occur quite frequently in early Hebrew (cf. Gen. 6:7; 9:9; Ex. 14:7, etc.). In 13:2 the construct chain is broken by the introduction of מ as follows: לִנְבִיאֵי מִלִּבָּם , which may show Aramaic influence, but similar particles are introduced in Hebrew breaking the chain (cf. שמחה בצפריה).

Finally, C.C. Torrey points out that the interrogative particle ה is often absent in Ezekiel (cf. 11:13; 17:9; 18:13, 24; 33:26).[49] It is well to remember that the particle is often missing in Hebrew as well as in Aramaic. The interrogative particle continues to occur in Biblical Aramaic and in the Targum, which makes it impossible to assume that the absence of it points to Aramaic.

Syntactical Aramaisms in Ez. are non-existent; however, mixed syntax would hardly be expected from one who knew both Hebrew and Aramaic.

Conclusion

The evidence for Aramaic influence in Ezekiel has been carefully surveyed. On the basis of the above material what conclusions can be drawn concerning the language? There is definite Aramaic influence felt in vocabulary and morphology, but the extent of such Aramaizing is far smaller than Selle would lead the casual reader of his study to believe. Egyptian, general Northwest Semitic, Hebrew, seventh century B.C. Aramaic have all been lumped together by Selle and others with the label "late Aramaic" on them. Many scholars seem quick to refer any difficult word or form to Aramaic, which is too easy a way out of difficulty.

Aramaic syntactical influence is negligible in Ezekiel, and not even by the wildest stretch of the imagination can the book be considered as written in any tongue but Hebrew. True, the Hebrew differs from that of Isaiah, but is there a language which does not change in a period of a century and a half, especially when such a language is spoken in a region where it is subject to all sorts of outside influences? In the light of all the evidence discussed in this chapter, the following statement by Torrey should be carefully reconsidered:
> The language of the book is not only late, it is very late. The significant change in the literary Hebrew certainly appears here to have progressed distinctly beyond what we observe in the writings of the Chronicler. The stage of development is more nearly that which is illustrated in Daniel, Esther, and Ecclesiastes.[50]

Kropat's study of the Chronicler's language and Curtis' list of late words in Chronicles show that work to be beyond question very much later than Ezekiel. The Chronicler's work is filled with Aramaic loan words and forms, also the syntax often shows clearly that the writer has lapsed into Aramaic construction and word-order instead of Hebrew.[51] There is no comparison to be drawn between the extensive Aramaizing in Chronicles and rare occurrences in Ezekiel, most of which are scribal. Torrey's comparison of the language of Ezekiel with that of Ecclesiastes is most disconcerting. In a recent article he maintained that Ecclesiastes is a late Hebrew translation of an earlier Aramaic work.52 We are not yet ready to accept this hypothesis, but it is freely admitted that the language of Ecclesiastes is very late. Again, a comparison of the language of Ezekiel on the one hand and that of Ecclesiastes on the other proves that the latter is very much later than the former.

Our resulting picture of the Aramaic in Ezekiel is very clear. To be sure, there is a small amount of Aramaic influence in the book, largely consisting of loan words, a few verb forms and noun endings with practically no evidence of syntactical influence. The nature of "the Aramaizing" leads us to the conclusion that it results mostly from scribal errors made by copyists who knew more Aramaic than Hebrew, probably an Aramaic-speaking scribe or scribes during the Babylonian Exile. Such persons in producing early copies of the book unintentionally allowed certain Aramaisms to get into the text. At the time of the writing or copying the scribes had been in Babylon at least thirty years, which is quite long enough for the local speech to have had its effect. After the prophet's death Babylonian Jewish scribes continued to copy the text, perhaps until after the Restoration. With each copy new Aramaisms were added, but the remarkable fact is that there are not more. The language not only substantiates the traditional date of the book, it also lends support to the Babylonian residence of the prophet. A tendency toward Aramaizing would not have been nearly so great had the prophet been a resident of Jerusalem all of the time, as illustrated by the almost total absence of Aramaisms in Hebrew books of early post-Exilic Palestinian origin. The language points to a sixth century B.C. date in a Babylonian locale.53

Chapter IV

PSYCHOLOGICAL ASPECTS OF EZEKIEL AND HIS PROPHECY

FOR CENTURIES readers of Ezekiel's book have been impressed by the fact that its author was a man of unusual temperament and powers. He was a visionary who saw strange, unheard of sights and couched the description of them in weird apocalyptic language. At times the prophet was subject to seizures which struck him silent and led to bizarre but meaningful symbolic actions. Added to this was his almost unprecedented ability to see "spaceless visions," that is, to be in one place and at the same time behold events faraway. As if this were not a great enough talent for one prophet, he displays also a power over individuals in these distant places (11:13). Actually his prophetic word was potent enough to bring about the death of a man even when that man was miles away from the scene of the oracle. These strange powers and unusual actions lead a reader to feel that Ezekiel was no ordinary personality.

Some overly-devout exegetes are quick to defend the prophet's normality and completely disallow deviation from their norms of human conduct. To try to maintain such a position is to fly directly in the face of the facts. The "norm" is a statistical abstract from which every person more or less deviates.[1] The genius not only of Ezekiel but of all great Hebrew prophets is to be found in this very fact, that they were not normal human beings.[2]

It is, however, unfortunate that the language and actions of Ezekiel's prophecy have provided a happy hunting ground for those with a little knowledge of psychology. We do not deny for a moment that psychology may very well be the vehicle through which many of the prophetic "deviations from the norm" may be tentatively explained, but trying to psychoanalyze at such a distance is dangerous.

There have been other efforts to probe our prophet's subconscious, but the latest and most thoroughgoing effort was made by Edwin C. Broome in his article titled, "Ezekiel's Abnormal Personality."[3] The conclusion of this "psychologistic" discussion is that Ezekiel was afflicted with catatonic or paranoid schizophrenia. Before trying to understand Broome's discussion it is necessary to refresh the reader's mind about the nature and symptoms of those mental diseases which are ordinarily grouped under the covering term schizophrenia.

The term schizophrenia is employed to designate several personality disorders, not just a single abnormal phenomenon. However, there is a series of symptoms which recur in the various forms of the disease. The outstanding symptoms of schizophrenia are: (a)Lack of logical thinking and feeling; (b)Apathy and absence of feeling; (c)Strange and incongruous actions; (d)Seclusiveness and extreme introversion; (e)Irrelevant and incoherent speech patterns; (f)Delusional thinking and hallucinations; (g) Neglect of conduct and personal habits. These are the general symptoms which may appear in the various types of schizophrenia but certainly no one case would include them all. For a more complete discussion reference should be made to Thorpe and Katz.[4]

For clinical purposes schizophrenia has been divided into four types: (a)the simple, (b)the hebephrenic, (c)the catatonic and (d)the paranoid. This classification, though inadequate in many ways, is widely accepted for practical reasons.[5] Cameron prefers the classifications (a)aggressive, (b)submissive and (c)detached,[6] but we choose to follow the more generally used four-category classification. Needless to say, there is great overlapping in the symptoms shown in any given patient since he may display features of more than one of these types.

A person suffering from simple schizophrenia first shows waning interest in his surroundings and seeks solitude by withdrawing from family and other social relationships. Then he begins to daydream and have fanciful thoughts. Such an individual often remains in one position for unbelievably long periods of time with a set expression on his face. Generally in cases of simple schizophrenia, there is no intellectual impairment; the individual is oriented and he seldom suffers either from hallucinations or delusions.

Hebephrenic schizophrenia is more severe than the simple type. Here again apathy and seclusiveness are typical symptoms at the onset of the illness. Inappropriate laughter and giggling, grotesque grimaces, purposeless mannerisms and abnormal speech mark its development. Delusions and hallucinations are common to the patient who is aware of illogical "mystery machines" and hears strange voices. A man thus afflicted loses control of his emotions which vacillate from convulsive laughter to frenzied crying and to explosive fits of anger.

Catatonic schizophrenia is distinguished from other types by the motor activity of the patient. He may display either a stuporous lack of activity or an excited continuous activity or he may vacillate between the two. In the stuporous phase the

the patient may refuse to speak, to eat, to dress, or to eliminate. He usually assumes an awkward waxlike position for long periods of time. Such a victim often remembers events which occurred during these cataleptic states. On the other hand, in the excited stage of catatonia the afflicted shows frenzied motor activity, reflected in fits of rage.

Paranoid schizophrenia is in many ways the most severe type exhibited in the conflicting delusions of grandeur and persecution. These delusions are usually illogical and grotesque. Such a person feels that others are talking about him, trying to poison him or seeking his hurt in innumerable ways. Hallucinations may be auditory, visual or somatic, with auditory, taste and smell predominating.[7]

With this introduction to schizophrenia in general and the disease classified under that term specifically we are now in a better position to understand Broome's treatment of "Ezekiel's Abnormal Personality."

At the very beginning Broome accepts Buttenwieser's theory that Ezekiel never prophesied before 586 B.C., hence his predictions are all post eventum.[8] Of Buttenwieser's explanation he says: "The position appears to me to be quite reasonable, and it disposes once and for all of clairvoyance, second sight, and the 'psychic' quality of the prophet's insight."[9] Still the reader is promised a better way to get rid of clairvoyance and other bothersome prophetic powers.

It is pointed out that the first outward indications of a psychosis are more or less bizarre in form; the patient may feel that a sinister person or force is out to "get him." He sometimes assumes a position, remaining motionless and mute over long periods of time. The first such symptom in Ezekiel is mentioned in 3:15f. where the prophet speaks of dwelling "overwhelmed" (שׁמם) among the exiles in Babylon. By divine command he is made responsible for warning his fellow countrymen about their impending doom (3:16-21). However, he is told that upon arrival in the midst of these folk they will restrain him with bands (3:25). By radical editing and rearrangement the original picture, as Broome sees it, is restored. The verses must be properly placed in the following order: 3:15, 3:24, 4:4-5, 4:8, 3:26. Double reference to Ezekiel's being put in "bands" (3:25 by the people, 4:8 by Yahweh) indicates either that Ezekiel had become so dangerous as to necessitate confinement or he believed himself "bound." In either case he was psychotic.[10]

Broome correctly points out that amnesia is not a regular

part of the catatonic state, hence there is nothing incredible about Ezekiel's remembering the visionary details.[11] The acts described in Ez. 4-5 came about only in catatonia and never actually occurred in reality. Attention should be directed especially to the revolting picture of human or animal excrement being used as fuel, an act very much like the soiling of the analsadistic stage of regression.[12]

"The thirtieth year" definitely refers, according to Broome, to the age of the prophet and is a symptom of his malady. The prophet places great emphasis on his age as being important to remember. This sort of thinking is typical of a man with delusions of grandeur. In 1:3 אל יחזקאל is read and היה היה is retained as further proof of the grandiose delusions of Ezekiel. "The word of Yahweh came expressly unto me, Ezekiel." In other words, Ezekiel felt himself singled out from the rest of the race as the recipient of a unique vision, vouchsafed to no other mortal.[13] Later in the Valley of Dry Bones (Ez. 37) and the Gog and Magog visions (Ez. 38-39) the prophet exhibits the same delusion of grandeur. By use of words the prophet causes the slain to rise and with the same instrument is able to slay the forces of Gog and Magog.[14]

At this point Broome begins to follow a strictly Freudian line in his interpretation of evidence drawn from the text. The fire vision of chapter 1 is essentially an anxiety symbol and reflects the nameless terror which Ezekiel was facing.[15] The meanings of various figures in the merkabah of chapter 1 are unknown. However, we can be sure that the fire and animal faces together add up to some powerful anxiety. The moving nude feminine figures (חיות) flitting to and fro give more force to the suggestion of a deep-seated anxiety.[16]

There is a conflict between the narcissistic and the masochistic tendencies in the prophet, thus making a definite psychosis. He is persecuted, haunted by the awesome eyes and the חשמל which, according to Broome, was probably a great bronze eye. By a sense of self-importance the prophet seeks unsuccessfully to combat the haunting, pursuing, accusing eyes.[17] Finally a voice speaks and he hears the sound of rushing waters. These of course are symbolic birth waters, showing that Ezekiel wishes to regress to prenatal security. The appearance of light destroys this unconscious security and leaves Ezekiel completely helpless.[18]

Broome further recognises in "the chariot" of the first chapter an "influencing machine," which is a very common psychic phenomenon in the delusions of those suffering from paranoid schizophrenia. Naturally the prophet's machine would have great theological significance. Ezekiel, like other schizophrenics, changes the details of the chariot, making the face of an animal into a cherub's face, but it remains essentially the same influencing machine.[19]

A most interesting point in Broome's psychologizing is his interpretation of סרבים (briers) and סלונים (thorns) as indicating the stinging, pricking sensation complained of by patients afflicted with schizophrenia.[20] Since Ezekiel was afflicted by סרבים and סלונים, he must have been experiencing the same abnormal sensation.

The eating of the scroll (2:9-3:3) is a definite unconscious sexual perversion and the symbol of the sharp sword in chapter 5 points to a desire on the part of the prophet to castrate himself. The hole dug through the Temple wall, revealing all sorts of abominations, is, according to Broome, another similar sexual perversion (8:7-13). In fact the whole event is terrible to the prophet because he feels at that point like a woman.[21]

Further symptoms are seen in the word שמיר (3:8-9), usually translated "adamant" but probably meaning here a "thornlike pain" in the forehead, which pain is common among schizophrenics. Ezekiel's identification of Jaazaniah and Pelatiah as arch-conspirators against God and His people indicates his unbalanced mental condition (8:11, 11:1, 13).[22] Finally the repetition of the inaugural vision of chapter 1 in chapter 10 is typical of the recurrent phantasies experienced by such people.[23]

After making these points Broome indicates that a schizophrenic could still make a significant contribution to religion. While a victim of such a malady he might also show real political and social wisdom. It is, therefore, not impossible to accept Ezekiel as a great religious, social and political leader even though he was mentally sick.

Ezekiel exhibits the following symptoms of schizophrenia: (a) periods of catatonia, (b) the delusion of an influencing machine, (c) a narcissistic-masochistic conflict, with attendant phantasies of castration and sexual regression, (d) schizophrenic withdrawal, (e) delusions of persecution and grandeur. Thus the prophet becomes classified as a definite paranoid schizophrenic.[24]

Before turning to a discussion of this article point by point a few general observations would be useful as background.

It is most remarkable, to our way of thinking at least, that a non-professional student of psychiatry and psychology should claim success in psychoanalyzing an individual who has been dead for 2500 years. Accuracy in such a venture would be quite unbelievable even if detailed autobiographical and biographical material were available. However, the claim of an ability to psychoanalyze a man about whose life we have only the vaguest and most general hints is completely out of the question.

We should remind ourselves also that the competent psychiatrist needs a relatively complete case history of family and social background before he begins direct interviews. At least six interviews face to face with the patient are required before preliminary diagnosis can be given. Needless to say, there are neither personal nor family records available to form a background for the case history of Ezekiel. It goes without saying that interviews can hardly be held. The small bits of information found in his book are not at all clear, since the terminology grew out of a social and religious background which we are unable to reconstruct. His strange words and ideas may not have been important deviations from "the norm" established for that time.[25]

In fairness to Broome his arguments should be reviewed more closely and more in detail. Broome's rearrangement of the text (i.e., 3:15; 3:24; 4:4-5; 4:8; 3:26) in order to bring the prophetic material in line with a prearranged scheme is without any real objective basis. Should scholarship finally succumb to such subjective treatment of textual material, we might soon have well worked out "case histories" for many ancient figures.

We do not know what "the bands" meant to Ezekiel. It is entirely possible, even probable, that there was definite objection, even among the gôlāh, to the prophet's constant denunciation. Such a conclusion is plausible when we remember the rather violent reaction from this same group to Jeremiah's unsolicited advice (Jer. 29). A prophet who constantly shattered the hopes for restoration which were cherished by exiles might well end up in literal bands. As for the bands that Yahweh put on the prophet (4:8), there is nothing so psychopathic about this concept when it is interpreted in the particular religious and social milieu of which Ezekiel was a part. Having said all this, however, exactly what is meant by "the bands" must remain an unsolved problem.

The fact that Ezekiel sat "overwhelmed" (שמם) for seven days is not unlikely even for a normal person under such circumstances. His country was destroyed, he was a captive and the future was very dark. Small wonder that a sensitive soul should feel desolate amid such terrible conditions.

One must agree with Broome, on the basis of modern authoritative psychiatric data, that a patient in a state of catatonia might remember details of events transpiring during a seizure. As one authority says: "In this stuporous state the individual appears to be entirely oblivious to what is going on around him. There have, however, been instances in which stuporous patients, under improvement, have reported events which occurred during such a period."[26] Further we are in agreement with Broome that chapters 4 and 5 are visionary, but whether the prophet carried out any or all the divine visionary directives is not known. This subject will be treated below.

Did Ezekiel really have delusions of grandeur? The assumption that "the thirtieth year" refers to the prophet's age is completely untenable, as we have shown in chapter II. Furthermore, there is no textual evidence for reading אֱלִ֫י הֲרָא אֱלָא for אֲרָא הֲרָא אֱלָא. On the other hand הַיָּה הָיֹה, on the basis of Syriac, Targum and Vulgate, should be read הָיָה or with the LXX וַיְהִי. In any case, the present reading represents a horizontal dittography, and one of the variant readings must be correct. By examining "the critical technique" of Broome an <u>argumentum in circulo</u> is revealed. Beginning with the assumption that the prophet did have delusions of grandeur, Broome forces "the thirtieth year" to fit the pattern, testimony to the contrary not withstanding. Then without textual evidence he alters אֱלָא to אֵלַי in order to further his hypothesis. But to our utter amazement, when the text calls for a change in reading, he rejects the evidence in order not to damage his case. Having tailored the text to fit his theory, the emended reading is then used to prove the original assumption which led to emendation in the first place.

It is not our purpose to discuss here the whole Freudian concept of personality, especially since criticisms of this hypothesis by competent students of psychology are available. We should do well to remember that a symbol must be interpreted in a specific historical context and in the light of allied events. Fire, for example, was traditionally connected by the Israelites with visions of Yahweh. Abraham's theophany (Gen.15: 17) was accompanied by fire; Moses saw a burning bush (Ex.3:2); there was fire on Sinai (Ex. 19:16-19); Elijah was taken from earth in a chariot of fire (II Kgs. 2:11); fire was definitely a part of Isaiah's call to prophecy (Is. 6); and on many other occasions a vision of Yahweh was in some way related to the idea of fire. With such a long symbolic tradition we should expect "fire" to have a place in Ezekiel's vision without any special anxiety being indicated. Moreover, the vision of chapter 1 may well have had the dramatic natural setting of a thunderstorm, thus giving rise to the appearance of fire (lightning). The constant movement of "the living creatures" would be part and parcel of a vision experienced in the midst of a real storm. Needless to say, neither Broome nor anyone else knows whether or not the חיות were nude or feminine. Of course, lack of definite information leaves the way open for an interpretation in keeping with previous psychological assumptions.

From the earliest times in exegesis of Ezekiel's book great interest has been shown in the weird <u>merkabah</u> (heavenly chariot) described in chapter 1. Broome, however, thinks he has at last found the solution to its source. "Influencing machines" are common to the visionary and mental processes of schizophrenics, and this is, he believes, clearly just such a machine. The exact meaning of the various parts of the machine are unknown to us, but they represent distortions of things seen by the prophet in conscious experience. This vision is extremely hard to understand, and we must admit that the exact nature of the <u>merkabah</u> is beyond explanation. So cryptic is the whole passage that one does well to avoid drawing definite conclusions. It is probable that the whole vision would be explicable if we knew more about the circumstances under which Ezekiel experienced it.

It is later stated by Broome that schizophrenics often change details of their "influencing machines" as Ezekiel alters the face of an ox to that of a cherub (cf. 10:14). The stuff of which visions are made is always quite fluid, hence this change is to be expected since both cherubim and oxen had religious significance. Identification of the <u>merkabah</u> with an "influencing machine" is very improbable.

Ezekiel's psychosis is said to be derived from his delusions of grandeur (narcissistic) on the one hand and his feeling of persecution (masochistic) on the other. He is haunted by the eyes in "the wheels" and the great חשמל "eye," also pursuing him. There is no hint, however, in the text that these eyes were haunting or persecuting him nor is there one whit of reason for taking חשמל to be another larger eye. Once Ezekiel has been driven to an extremity, he hears a voice like waters. These waters are, we learn, the symbol of birth waters and betray the prophet's desire for a return to the safety of the pre-natal condition. If this vision took place in the midst of a storm, as we believe it did, then would the natural phenomenon of falling waters have psychic significance? We point to the usage of "waters" (47:1-12) which definitely represent the life-giving qualities of water in a desert and could hardly have anything to do with "birth-waters."

The rather difficult terms סרבים (briers) and סלונים (thorns) are forced into the pattern. They are said to represent the stinging, pricking sensation commonly experienced by those in this state. One wonders if the man who is able to propose this theory has ever heard of figurative expressions used both in ancient and modern times.

Of course, with Freud sex is the basic drive in human life, and Broome certainly follows "the party line" completely. Eating of the scroll (2:9-3:3) represents the worst sort of sexual perversion, a conclusion largely drawn from the shape of the scroll. Obvious and important symbolism known to be connected with the scroll is overlooked. Worse yet is the symbol of the sword (Ez. 5), which betrays the prophet's desire to castrate himself. In ancient times the sword represented the destruction of warfare, not of emasculation. The warped sexual makeup of the prophet is further revealed by the sexual act of digging a hole in the wall and beholding abominations of an unbelievable kind (8:7-13). Why could not the digging of such a hole represent no more than the vision of a common process which was actually carried out in chapter 12? We are rather disappointed that a Freudian explanation of the removal (cf. Ez. 12) has not been given us, for that would have been most interesting.

Broome's guesswork on שמיר is definitely born of a desire to establish his theory. Indeed if one must go this far to establish an idea, his theory is proved very weak indeed. Even if שמיר did mean "a headache," how could a modern scholar possibly know it without lexicographical evidence (of which there is none). The word carried over into Aramaic with the meaning "diamond", but there is no trace of Broome's unusual translation.

It should be stated here that there undoubtedly existed men like Pelatiah and Jaazaniah, who were responsible in part for the sad state of affairs in Jerusalem. Just because the prophet became their accuser does not automatically classify him with schizophrenics. Basic to such a conclusion is the assumption that Pelatiah and Jaazaniah, if they existed, were innocent of the prophetic charges leveled at them. Not only on this point but on others Broome shows a complete lack of appreciation for the historical situation. The revolting picture in 4:15 of a captive preparing meals with animal manure as fuel probably represents reality within a besieged city, not the "soiling propensities" typical of schizophrenic regression. Actually the modern Arabs still commonly use dried animal dung for fuel. In both cases Broome fails to understand the situation that actually existed.[27]

The hearing of voices was a common psychic experience in Hebrew history, for it was by hearing a voice that all great prophets had been called into divine service. For a man who had grown up near the Temple and under the influence of the tradition of his people, we should expect some such expression for that inexpressible feeling of the presence of God. Today a great majority might question the sanity of a man who claims to have heard the heavenly voice, but such claims were rather common in Ezekiel's day. In other words, this whole study of the prophet judges him against a modern backdrop, not against a setting of the sixth century B.C.

Once Freudian symbols are accepted as completely valid for all ages, then human action must stem from an unconscious perversion of the sex instinct. However, few psychiatrists today accept sex as the only drive of life and very few would insist that Freud's symbols can be used without reference to a given historical context. There is still much to be learned about the "inner life of man" from the psychological point of view, but it is hardly to be hoped that we shall ever find it possible accurately to interpret the inner life of a man long departed and about whom we know so very little.

In each of us there may well be found certain schizophrenic symptoms, and of course, they were not wholly absent in Ezekiel or any other ancient prophet. Granting that these symptoms do appear in all men, a scholar who assumes a given psychopathic condition can by picking and choosing convincingly show that an individual of ancient times was mentally unbalanced. That is precisely what Broome has done with Ezekiel. His critical emendations leave something to be desired, and his lexicographical method is most disconcerting.

One point of tremendous importance has completely escaped the attention of Broome in his remarkable investigation of Ezekiel's "inner life." Cameron points out that a day dreamer can return from the world of fantasy to normal role taking but the schizophrenic cannot.[28] We maintain that Ezekiel was a daydreamer par excellence and not a schizophrenic since he often returned to the Tel-Abib community as a well-oriented, helpful member of society. Always he was in general touch with reality. His visions of Jerusalem were in definite, though general, contact with the situation which developed there. Ezekiel was a visionary who never strayed far from the practical situation and whose abnormality gave him a remarkable insight into current events.[29]

Hines has made a fine contribution to our understanding of Ezekiel's personality by his article comparing our prophet with well known mystics.[30] Buttenwieser and more recently Widengren have used the same approach to this rather difficult subject.[31]

That Ezekiel was a visionary who is to be classed with the outstanding mystics of the world's great religions is clear. There are, according to Hines, five major visonary experiences of the prophet recorded in the prophecy as it now stands. They are: "(1)The Initial Call, 1:4-3:15; (2)The Vision of the Siege and Fall of Jerusalem, 3:22-5:17; (3)The Vision of the Abominations and Ruin of Jerusalem, chaps. 8-11; (4)The Vision of the Valley of Bones, 37:1-14; (5)The Vision of the Restored Temple and Land, chaps. 40-48."[32]

Hines' contention that 3:22-5:17 is visionary has received the support of Broome and others.[33] We accept this as a logical explanation of the impossible feats which the prophet was ordered to carry out. No doubt some of the commands given in the vision actually took place in reality, but just which ones were enacted we are not able to say. It would be well to remember that in the mind of the visionary it is very difficult to differentiate between real actions and visionary experiences. Hence this problem of the extent to which divine orders were literally carried out must forever remain an unanswered question.

Before discussing the visions individually we shall review the parallels between Ezekiel and other mystics, as presented by Hines and others.

Buttenwieser draws his illustrations of ecstatic visionary activity from reports in classical literature where voyages to heaven and hell are rather common among those "inspired." Aristeas of Proconnesus (sixth century B.C.) is said to have been subject to long ecstatic seizures during which he would travel in the form of a raven to distant places. Another mystic of ancient Greece was Hermotimus of Clazomenae, whose soul would wander in ecstatic flights and then return to his body. After such a flying experience, he would be able to reveal knowledge absolutely unattainable by any normal method. Added to this list are the ascetic Epimenides of Crete (mentioned in Plato's *Republic*) and Arrhidaeus (recorded by Plutarch). In every case these ecstatics were easily transported from one place to another while in a visionary trance, and upon return to normality they were able to verify their travels by detailed descriptions of places visited. Of course, these examples are second-hand reports of mystic experiences and may be discounted on the grounds of inaccurate recording.34

Hines presents more recent, first-hand examples of the same sort of mystical personality and activity. St. Teresa in her initial vision tells how she saw Christ "with the eyes of the soul." He was very close to her and spoke with her in a reassuring voice which calmed her fears and gave her comfort. Essentially the same vision was repeated at a later time by Teresa. On another occasion she tells of a vision which came while she was at prayer. In this mystic state she was "transported to Hell, saw the horror, felt the anxiety, sadness and dispair of the inmates." The experience moved her to devote the rest of her life to bringing about the salvation of souls and to delivering them from hell. The whole mystical trip is not only like those referred to in classical writings but bears a remarkable resemblance to Ezekiel's vision in chapters 8-11.35

Suso, a German mystic who lived in the fourteenth century A.D., was subject to the same visionary trances. At thirteen he became a Dominican monk and studied at the University of Cologne, where he was about to be awarded the degree of doctor of theology when a vision of God came to him. The divine voice said: "Thou knowest well enough already to give voice to God and to draw men to Him by thy preaching." Immediately he became a great preacher and a teacher of the mystic way. Many of his experiences were written down and circulated by a friend. When Suso found this out, he began to have them destroyed. Only another vision halted the destruction of this record.36

Alone one day in the choir on St. Agnes day he saw a great vision. Hines describes the mystic sight as follows:
Suddenly he saw and heard what no tongue could express. It was without form or being and yet had within itself the joy of all forms and all manner of beings. It was at the same time the totality of desire and of accomplishment in the forgetfulness of everything and of self. It was the happiness of eternal life in rest and silence.37

Even Ezekiel's initial vision is more clearly described than this unearthly experience of Suso, yet the visions of the two men have much in common.

Finally, the case of Al-Ghazzali is to the point. A brilliant intellectual career had not given him the deep satisfaction which he sought, so he deserted family and fame to become a Sufi and found happiness in mystical transport. He was able to write lucidly about the nature of these visionary trances, describing the experience as "immediate perception" of that which is beyond the normal life.[38] These unearthly travels of mystics may bear them to distant parts of the universe, to heaven or hell, or even into the presence of God Himself.

Ezekiel's experience is far from being unique, for mystics in all ages have shared in the same sort of visionary life which he claims for himself. His transport from one place to another, his vision of God, his commission and many other factors are found in the lives of numerous mystics of the great religions. With Hines we put the prophet and the mystic generally in the same psychological category, but mysticism and prophetism are not to be equated. The extreme form of mysticism in which the mystic becomes one with deity has no counterpart among the prophets. The prophet was the spokesman of Yahweh, but there remained a complete separation between God and man.[39]

The inaugural vision of the prophet (1:4-3:15) has been a source of great difficulty to many exegetes who have found it beyond interpretation. Cohon says of the prophet: "He saw things that never were and never could be, neither in the heavens above or on the earth below nor in the waters beneath the earth."[40] On the contrary, this vision is a reflection of conscious experience and background, for the unconscious does not manufacture its visions from nothing.[41] The vision is a refraction of real elements in Ezekiel's life and memory. Widengren in his recent book correctly recognises this distorted contact with reality in the magnificent visionary scene in chapter 1. The subconscious mind takes material from conscious life and builds it into something more than can be attained in conscious experience.[42] It is almost a truism of psychology that socio-religious background and environment determine the content of both the conscious and subconscious. Ezekiel is no exception to this established rule. Both Palestinian and Babylonian backgrounds can be clearly seen in his visions.

We must agree with Hines that 3:22-5:17 does not represent real activity but is a vision. It has been noted that when Ezekiel received a visionary command to action which was literally carried out, he recorded the fact. In the act of removal from the besieged city he says: "And I did so as I was commanded. ." (12:7a); and also on the occasion of his wife's death when he was told not to weep, he reports, ". . .I did in the morning as I was commanded." However, there is no such statement made with reference to the visions of 3:22-5:17.

82   THE DATE AND COMPOSITION OF EZEKIEL

Chapters 8-11 are probably to be taken as one vision which Ezekiel experiences just as he reports it. He was transported to Jerusalem, where he saw general scenes of religious syncretism, political unrest and social decay. In this vision he denounces the activities of Pelatiah so vehemently that the denunciation kills the object of his wrath. This potency of the prophetic word over long distances has posed a serious problem for students of Ezekiel in modern times.

It has long been assumed that the syncretistic worship of chapter 8 must have been taking place concurrently with the prophecy given in Babylon. This does not follow at all. For by the same reasoning process it would be necessary for us to conclude that Jerusalem was laid waste at precisely the moment when the prophet had his vision of the destroyer (cf. Ez. 9). Chapter 8 represents a general condemnation and denunciation of religious practices which had been common in Judah since the death of Josiah. Notice that "general denunciation." This is a very important point, for not once in the chapter is an exact detail given which could not have been known to the prophet. Ezekiel's information undoubtedly came primarily from the memory of similar scenes during his residence in Palestine and late news of these religious trends received via some sort of grape vine. That these activities were occurring often was certain, but we hardly think that the prophet is describing specific incidents.[43]

Chapter 10 is the sort of vision within a vision which one would expect under these circumstances. God is abandoning an evil and undeserving city which is doomed to destruction.

The real problem arises in connection with chapter 11, more especially with Pelatiah's death being inflicted by the prophetic word. We feel that Buttenwieser has come closer to solving this problem than any other scholar in recent times. He feels that Pelatiah did die and ten years later Ezekiel connected his imaginary prophecy with this dramatic incident in a cause and effect pattern.[44] Our agreement with Buttenwieser is not complete because we maintain that the visionary prophecy was real. However, as we shall later attempt to show, Ezekiel had his book recorded in the thirtieth year of the captivity. At that time he remembered that Pelatiah died on the occasion of the denunciation against him and other leaders of Jerusalem's people was being given. All the prophet says is: "And it came to pass when I prophesied, that Pelatiah the son of Benaiah died . . ."(11:13a). Whether this is cause and effect might be questioned. The verse looks very much like a later addition to a vision which would be quite complete without it. When the record was made, Ezekiel added this dramatic event, the news of which reached him at his Babylonian home.

Clairvoyance has long been a bone of contention among scholars who have studied Ezekiel's book because in chapters 8 and 11 there seemed to be clear examples of this unusual gift. Those who did not admit the possibility of clairvoyance denied that the prophet was in Babylon. It appears to us that we do not have a clear case of clairvoyance anywhere in Ezekiel, especially in the chapters under discussion. This conclusion is not forced upon us by any unwillingness to accept clairvoyance as a possible fact. It is our sincere hope that psychological experiments will one day confirm or rule out once for all this strange power. Ezekiel did not see detailed events simultaneously with their occurrence, but reflected on the general movement of forces at work on a distant scene. This is not true clairvoyance.[45]

The Vision of the Valley of Dry Bones and the Vision of the Temple and Land Restored round out the major visionary experiences of Ezekiel. Both are unconscious representations of conscious experiences. On his way into captivity the young priest must have seen fields strewn with the bones of fallen warriors who tried unsuccessfully to stop the Chaldean advance. From there his imagination fashioned the vision. What more natural dream or mystical vision could one of priestly lineage have than that of the Temple restored? On the fourteenth anniversary of the city's destruction this picture of the future would naturally come to one who was thoroughly acquainted with the Temple environs and who even on this tragic date was thinking of the Temple that had been. Psychologically the date is perfect for the vision described in 40-48.

We do not have the necessary information to understand chapters 38-39, but it is safe to say in passing that Gog and Magog probably represent that age-old fear of attack from the north. It was from that direction that terrible hordes had poured into the Fertile Crescent since the dawn of history.

Ezekiel was a mystical individual with a sensitive spirit caught in the cross-currents of history. Hines claims correctly that Ezekiel's oracles are derived from three major factors:
> . . .(a)the instinctive struggles of himself and his fellow exiles to adjust to their new situation under tense mental strain, (b)the environmental thought and religious life of his milieu and (c)the sensitivity of his artistic temperament. . .[46]

In other words, a young priest was suddenly snatched from the security of the Temple in Jerusalem and carried away captive to Babylon. There in new surroundings he saw sights of greater splendor and magnitude than anything found in Palestine. Contradictions appeared in the situation which had to be harmonized and which put a terrible strain on the prophet's sensitive spirit. Within him was the sure knowledge that Judah and Jerusalem were lost. Where was hope? In this historical context small wonder that a mystic should find some of the answers in visions.[47]

Kittel calls the prophet a child of two worlds: Babylon and Palestine; but more than that he maintains that there were "two souls in one breast."[48] That is, on the one hand, the pedantic priestly soul given to details of liturgy and law and on the other, the fire of the prophet who denounced the people, promising divine destruction for their sins.[49] Kittel is on the right track but has nearly made a schizophrenic of the prophet. Ezekiel had within himself the priestly and prophetic tendencies, but they seldom came into real conflict. The situation called for a critical appraisal of institutionalism but not a complete denunciation of it, for the future of the Jewish religion depended on the preservation of purified institutions. In Ezekiel there is a harmony of priest and prophet.

Ezekiel was not a schizophrenic incapable of normal roletaking but was rather a visionary, more akin to a daydreamer than to a mystic. Daydreamer is hardly a fitting description for this man who ranks with the world's great prophets. He was a mystic by nature with a sensitive, artistic imagination which brought forth some of the best known visions and symbolic figures of speech in Biblical literature. The Exilic prophet was not gifted with clairvoyance as some have held but saw in his visions general activity which was the result of widely known political and religious trends. In him the priestly and prophetic spirits found harmony.

In conclusion, therefore, Ezekiel was a sensitive, mystical individual caught in a great crosscurrent of history. He deviated considerably from "the norm" but was not truly psychopathic. No prophet is "normal" else he would not be a prophet. Ezekiel's strangeness or abnormality would seem to be the secret of his greatness. As W.F. Albright remarks: "Ezekiel was one of the greatest spiritual figures of all time, in spite of his tendency to psychic abnormality —a tendency he shares with many other spiritual leaders of mankind."[50] Our prophet was different from the common run of mankind, for to him had appeared a vision of Yahweh, whose servant he was.

Chapter V

THE COMPOSITION OF THE PROPHECY OF EZEKIEL

THE ORACLES and visions of Ezekiel are well ordered and chronologically arranged —a feature unique among the prophetic books of the Old Testament. Jeremiah exhibits neither chronological nor thought order, and Isaiah is more an anthology of many works than the writing of one author. In bold contrast Ezekiel has not only a definite chronological arrangement, but the book also possesses a progression in thought. Beginning with denunciation of a doomed community, the book reaches a climax with the vision of a restored temple and society at the end. Within the prophecy many investigators have seen what appeared to be the work of a single hand or at least the product of one mind. The book could be the work of a literary master who composed it during his leisure while being held captive among the Babylonians. For centuries, as we have noted above, this prophecy was considered to be the work of Ezekiel the prophet, but in recent years the problem of the composition of the book has become one of the central issues of Old Testament research.

R. Kraetzschmar, in an effort to preserve as genuine most of the book, in 1900 proposed the now well known two-recension theory of the text. He found at least twenty-three instances of alleged doublets in the text and suggested on this basis that two recensions of the book had once existed side by side: one in the first person and the other in the third person. Actually the material in the first person predominates so definitely that Kraetzschmar is forced to admit that the material from "the third-person recension" is no more than a short digest, being reflected directly only in 1:3 and 24:24. The two recensions, according to Kraetzschmar, were combined before the book was translated into Greek.[1]

J. Herrmann in his commentary on Ezekiel maintained strongly that the prophet in later life edited his earlier oracles, making additions and deletions at that time. Herrmann correctly recognised that the prophet did not complete this work at one sitting. There were editors and redactors who later worked on the text, but by and large the present prophecy was held to be the work of Ezekiel in the dual capacity as writer and editor.[2]

Both Herrmann and Kraetzschmar were influenced by a desire to preserve the greater part of Ezekiel's book for the traditional author. No such motivation can be detected in the commentary of Gustav Hölscher, who did a thorough pruning job. This radical German scholar took for granted that all genuine prophetic material in Ezekiel's book was poetic, having been written in a special qînāh metre. Furthermore, according to Hölscher, Ezekiel saw only two visions: the first was a call to prophesy (1:4, 28), and the second showed him the abominations of the temple environs (8:1-17, 9:1-7, 11:24, 25). His ministry was one of constant denunciation, unbroken by any ray of future hope. Oracles of doom were not leveled at Jerusalem alone, but also were directed against Tyre and Egypt in some of the most beautiful poetry of the whole book (27; 28:12-19; 30:21; 31:3-8; 32:2, 18-27). In all there are preserved in the book sixteen of the original prophetic oracles. The prose of the book and the passages of future hope were added by later redactors and editors in order to balance the rather violent words of Ezekiel himself. After Hölscher had done his work, there remained only about 170 verses which were ascribed to the prophet of the Babylonian gôlāh.3

We have already had occasion to discuss in detail the works of Torrey and Smith. Their theories, having to do mostly with date, failed to stand up under close critical scrutiny. Since date is the foundation stone of both efforts, their views on composition must be rejected along with the rejection of their dating.4

Irwin's book, The Problem of Ezekiel, is at once the latest and most arbitrary attempt at analysis of the text of this extremely difficult prophecy. By "induction" he arrives at certain "criteria" through which the genuine prophetic material can, according to him, be ferreted out. Irwin's method is plainly shown in the opening chapter of his book which lays down the "inductive foundation" for the remainder of his work. He selects Ez. 15 as the starting point of his study. The "genuine oracle" which, according to Irwin, is made up of verses 2 through 5 can immediately be recognised, but what of verses 6-8? They are a "false" commentary on the genuine material.5 In order to explain Irwin's unusual terminology we quote directly:
> This writer missed the main idea of the oracle that the vinewood is worthless; instead he snatched at the figure of the burning fire and so gave a totally diverse pronouncement. There is nothing in common between oracle and interpretation save their use of the symbols of vinewood and fire. The interpretation is false.6

Taking this "inductive" separation of the genuine from the spurious as a foundation, Irwin proposes a unique literary structure. For example, the introductory formula ויהי דבר יהוה

אל לאמר is genuine because it introduces the "genuine" oracles, but the word יען is clearly spurious since it is found in the "false" commentary, viz., vs. 6-8. In fact, according to him, the expression יען יכן became characteristic of later commentators, of whom there were many. In other passages Irwin succeeds in pointing out several other "spurious phrases" or words which, when found, mark the context as non-Ezekielian in origin. Nevertheless, it is often very difficult even for Irwin to separate the "genuine" from the "spurious" since the commentators often copied both the vocabulary and style of the great prophet. In spite of this rather formidable barrier Irwin is able by "inductive processes" to set up an "objective criterion" for separating genuine from spurious. Ezekiel was in fact a great poet, hence his real oracles are in poetic form. In this Irwin and Hölscher stand on the same ground, but Hölscher is severely criticized for not having arrived at the poetic measuring stick by Irwin's "inductive" method.[7]

The book of Ezekiel, as Irwin sees it, manifests a distinctive use of certain formulae and words and has a style characterized by short clear sketches. These short sketches are in poetic style as is evidenced by the genuine Oracle of the Vine in Ez. 15:2-5. Even in the long solid chapters of the prophecy the genuine oracle at the base of the long "false commentary" is extremely short. All Aramaic forms in the text are indicative of late, spurious additions to the genuine material. The priestly background of Ezekiel is false, and chapters 40-48 come from a much later hand. Gog and Magog must be dated after the era of Antiochus Epiphanes. To sum up, of the 1013 verses contained in Ez. 1-39 only 251 are in whole or part original with Ezekiel. The rest of the prophecy is "false commentary," reflecting many additions from a multitude of hands over a long period of time.[8]

Buttenwieser's theory about the book's composition rests largely on his interpretation of Ezekiel's dumbness. He points out that the prophet claims to have been dumb from 593 to 587 B.C. (3:27; 24:27;33:22), but an active prophetic ministry is described for that same period. Besides this, there is the difficulty raised by the remarkable accuracy of certain predictive oracles which were carried out almost to the letter. Buttenwieser decides, therefore, that Ezekiel was actually silent during the years 593 to 587 B.C. and that his real prophetic ministry began only after the city of Jerusalem had been laid waste. All the predictive oracles in Ez. 1-32 are prophecies after the fact.[9]

Kraetzschmar's work is very forceful, but many of his so-called doublets are not doublets at all. Where real doublets do occur there is usually a more logical explanation for them than "the two-recension" theory (see below). Two verses with the name Ezekiel in them do not offer very much evidence for a "third-person text" (1:3, 24:24), especially since these two verses probably represent the superscription and a subscription to the book, as we shall show later. Except for these two references there is not a single indication that a "third-person recension" ever existed.

Herrmann's book made a notable and lasting contribution to research on Ezekiel, a contribution which has in fact been enhanced by the passing years. His recognition that the prophetic book is really an anthology of Ezekiel's oracles from various dates must be accepted. Furthermore, Herrmann seems to be partly correct in naming the prophet as the editor of his own anthology of oracular material. We believe that Herrmann has come close to a suitable explanation of the composition but has overlooked a few important factors which we shall have opportunity to discuss later in this chapter.[10]

<u>Hesekiel, der Dichter und das Buch,</u> in which Hölscher does his remarkable analysis of the text, is by far the most thoroughgoing critical attack on the genuineness of the prophecy which has appeared to date. He makes two major assumptions from the outset: (a)Ezekiel was a prophet of doom, and (b)he was a poet. Hence any passage having to do with hope or couched in prose must automatically be declared spurious. Kessler has attacked Hölscher's work on the basis of an apparent inner unity which is exhibited between prose and poetry in the book. Such a relationship is very close in the prophecy, and it represents a very serious objection to Hölscher's view.[11]

Hölscher's premises seem to us very weak. How does he know that Ezekiel spoke and wrote only in qînāh metre? Is it not even probably that the highly emotional poetic style of the spoken oracle would become quite prosy when written down? Actually there is no reason for excluding prose from the book since a prophet of a priestly background might be more inclined to prose than other prophets without such a background.[12] We must also take issue with the assumption that Ezekiel was exclusively a prophet of doom since parallels from neighboring lands have proved that doom and hope did exist side-by-side in a given prophecy (cf. above).

Hölscher might be completely wrong in assuming that Ezekiel was primarily a poet because there is much more prose in the book than poetry and the poetry seems to be borrowed. That is

to say, Ezekiel was a poet but not an original one. He started
with well-known poetic models and refashioned them in such a
way as to carry his message effectively.[13] Chapter 15 is the
Parable of the Vine, which can hardly be original with our
prophet. The same can be said about the Oracle of the Green
Twig and the Eagles in 17 and the Picture of the Lioness and
Whelps in 19. These poems were probably widely known among the
people and provided excellent basic material for oracles on
the condition of king and people. The poem in 21:14-22 is possibly a refrain used in connection with some sort of sword
dance. Also, the figure of a cup in 23:32-34 is hardly original
with Ezekiel since essentially the same metaphor is found in
Jeremiah 25. Further evidence for this hypothesis is provided
by the poetic sections of the oracles against Tyre and Egypt
(parts of chapters 26-32). At the base of these oracles is a
poetic substructure which may have its real origin elsewhere,
not with Ezekiel. Similar poems about Egypt and Tyre, especially the descriptive sections, were undoubtedly in circulation
before the time of our prophet.[14]

Our hypothesis makes of Ezekiel a man who, like some of his
modern counterparts, used classical material as the basis for
his oracles. Sometimes this original material was in the form
of a story (e.g., Ez. 16 and 23), or at other times it took
proverbial shape (e.g., Ez. 18), but most often the core was a
poem from the past which was reinterpreted and made into a powerful lesson for the present. If our hypothesis be correct,
then the difference between the prose and poetry of the book
would be explained. Our suggestion is nothing more than an unproven theory, yet its plausibility does show that there is as
strong an a priori ground for such a position as for Hölscher's
analysis.

Irwin's "inductive" approach leads him to essentially the
same position which Hölscher reached in his book, except that
Irwin, by admitting that certain introductory formulae are genuine, is able to preserve as original about seventy-five more
verses than did Hölscher.[15] We begin our examination of Irwin's
explanation of the composition with chapter 15, where he began.
He takes verses 2-5 to be the original Oracle of the Vine,
which came from the lips of a great prophet-poet named Ezekiel.
Verses 6-8 are false commentary because they confuse the basic
vinewood metaphor with the idea of a destructive fire. This
misunderstanding of the original intent of the poem is to be
credited, according to Irwin, not to the prophet but is rather
a false commentary emanating from a later hand. We may observe
that throughout the ages men of vision have been breathing new
life into old forms and giving new interpretations to old

figures in spite of Irwin's assertion that Ezekiel could not rework and reinterpret old material.[16] The people were worthless like vinewood, hence they would be consumed by divine fire. Where is the false commentary in this very logical development? Irwin's case is founded on his analysis of this chapter; and since his work here is probably in error, his whole "inductive" scheme falls like a house of cards.[17]

The author of The Problem of Ezekiel is extremely dogmatic in saying that the priestly background of the book is spurious, that Gog and Magog follow the era of Antiochus Epiphanes and that the presence of Aramaic must indicate a late date for a given context.[18] Irwin discounts the priestly background of the book because he believes that Ezekiel must conform to a set prophetic pattern.[19] Although every prophet did follow a certain broad behavior pattern, each great prophet was an individualist whose peculiarities especially fitted him for the time during which he lived. Ezekiel's priestly leanings were very important to the formulation of a theocratic plan for the future. Gog and Magog are hard to understand, but whatever else may be said about them, of this we can be sure, there is nothing in these chapters which forces a late date upon them.[20] Concerning the language, we have already presented our interpretation of the Aramaic which occurs in the book.[21]

Buttenwieser's solution of the problem of composition rests squarely on the assumption that Ezekiel was silent prior to the Fall of Jerusalem. Undoubtedly there were periods following visionary journeys when Ezekiel sat "overwhelmed" by what he had seen. This could not have been a permanent thing, else how can we account for all of his spoken oracles during these years of silence? In 3:26 Yahweh promises that when He speaks to the prophet, his mouth will be opened. Upon returning from his visionary trip to Jerusalem (Ez. 8-11), he says: "Then I spoke to them of the captivity all the things which Yahweh had shown me" (11:25). He is told to "prophesy against the prophets of Israel" (13:1), to "put forth a riddle and speak a parable" (17:2a), to "speak unto the elders of Israel" (20:3a) and so the list could be extended. Were these all the inner ruminations of a silent man? That hardly seems possible since such an assumption would make it difficult to understand the great influence of Ezekiel's prophecy. Buttenwieser's desire to get rid of the predictive prophecy displayed by Ezekiel leads him to this solution, which makes all predictions post eventum. The references to dumbness must be explained in one of two ways: either they are figurative or they represent the period of silence which followed each visionary experience. The latter view is more convincing.[22]

None of these attempts at solution of the book's composition is satisfactory. Is there perhaps another explanation which will fit the facts in the case?

Our new analysis of the book starts at the beginning with the introductory verses. Torrey, among others, has recognised the great importance of "the thirtieth year" in verse 1, and it is with that date that our discussion is taken up. Spiegel, Albright and others have come to a most interesting conclusion about the enigmatic "thirtieth year."[23] It is their opinion that this date is a part of the scheme of the book, thus the verse has reference to the "thirtieth year" of Jehoiachin's captivity. This is quite logical, as we have shown above, since a change from the regular scheme of dating would have been specially noted, but an author would see no necessity for explaining a date which was in regular use throughout his writings. Moreover we have already seen that it is not necessary to synchronize this date with the one in verse 2 (see above) because the two are independent of each other. There may be a lacuna between them; possibly something has dropped out.[24]

These first verses resemble in many ways a regular superscription of a prophetic book. For comparative purposes we quote a few superscriptions from similar works.

The word of Yahweh that came to Hosea the son of Beeri, in the days of Uzziah, Jotham, Ahaz, and Hezekiah, kings of Judah, and in the days of Jeroboam the son of Joash, king of Israel. (Hos. 1:1)

The vision of Isaiah the son of Amoz, which he saw concerning Judah and Jerusalem in the days of Uzziah, Jotham, Ahaz and Hezekiah, kings of Judah. (Is. 1:1)

The words of Jeremiah the son of Hilkiah, of the priests that were at Anathoth in the land of Benjamin to whom the word of Yahweh came in the days of Josiah the son of Amon, the king of Judah, in the thirteenth year of his reign. (Jer. 1:1-2)

The words of Nehemiah the son of Hachaliah (Neh. 1:1a)

There are many others of which we might have taken note, but these are enough for comparison.[25] In each case the prophet's name is mentioned in the superscription along with that of his father. Besides this information the reader is also given the general dates for the prophet's ministry.

There is obviously some disarrangement in the first three verses of Ezekiel because early readers sought to synchronize

the dates in them. With Albright we rearrange them in some such way as the following: ויהי בשלשים שנה ברביעי בחמשה
לחדש(ו)היה דבר יהוה אל יחזקאל בן בוזי הכהן בארץ
כשדים על נהר כבר:(ו)בשנה החמשית לגלות המלך
יויכין בחמשה לחדש ואני בתוך הגולה על נהר כבר נפתחו
השמים ואראה מראות אלהים:ותהי עלי שם יד יהוה:וארא
> And it happened in the thirtieth year, in the fourth month, on the fifth day of the month that the word of the Lord came to Ezekiel, son of Buzi, the priest, on the river Chebar in the land of the Chaldeans: In the fifth year of the captivity of King Joiachin,<in the. . .month,> on the fifth day of the month while I was a member of the captivity on the river Chebar, heaven was opened, and I saw a divine vision. The hand of the Lord was on me there and I saw. . .[26]

This amounts to a rearrangement of clauses with little change in the text itself. We have a-e-d-c-b for a-b-c-d-e in clause order. The first היה is omitted with the versions; היא השנה is changed to בשנה because it is quite awkward in its present form.[27] Albright explains his reading thus:

> Our rearrangement of clauses is based on the intrinsic probability that the occurrence twice of the phrase בחמשה לחדש would cause the eye of the copyist to skip the intervening words and to continue from the second occurrence of the word in question. The other transpositions are the results of some later attempt to insert missing words which had been written on the margin in the right order.[28]

This rearrangement need not be correct in detail to point the way to the correct solution. The thirtieth year is then the time when Ezekiel first published his book. Perhaps the word "published" is misleading since by it we only mean that the book was dictated to a disciple or disciples who either wrote it down then or recorded it later from memory. It is our contention that most of the first twenty-four chapters are reminiscences of the prophet Ezekiel in the thirtieth year of the captivity of king Jehoiachin. In that year he probably received, as Spiegel thinks, a divine directive that a record of his oracles and visions was to be made. The written prophecies had one purpose: to drive home an important moral lesson of history, namely, "that they may know that I am the Lord Yahweh." Again and again this great theme sounds throughout the whole written prophecy![29]

There are two verses in Ezekiel that are written in the third person (1:3 and 24:24). These verses led Kraetzschmar to think that a "third-person recension" had once existed and that here we have a glimpse of the continuing abstract of that recension.[30] However, a close examination of the closing verses of chapter 24 gives one the impression that there is considerable confusion in the present order. We have already seen how 1:3, once the order is slightly altered, becomes a clear superscription. The second passage (viz. 24:24) similarly turns out to be in direct connection with the interpretation of the prophet's actions on the occasion of his wife's death.

> Thus shall Ezekiel be unto you a sign: according to all that he hath done shall ye do; when this cometh, then shall ye know that I am the Lord Yahweh. (24:24)

This indeed is an appropriate subscription to that part of the book which deals largely with the doom and coming destruction of Jerusalem (i.e., 1-24). Yet, the verse seems to be out of its proper order as it now stands. Its correct position would probably be at the end of the chapter, where a subscription would normally be expected. The verse in its present position clearly interrupts the thought progression besides changing from second to third person. This is not Ezekiel speaking!

For a fuller understanding of this disorder we must turn to chapter 33. As one reads this chapter, verses 21-22 appear to be misplaced, having no connection either with that which precedes them or with what follows. They have probably been transposed from some other section and placed here in the midst of unrelated oracles. These verses fit the end of chapter 24 naturally, and there we propose to put them. There is good reason for shifting 24:24 to the end of the passage following 33:21-22 since it is in fact a sort of subscription. Our reconstruction reads as follows in translation:

> (24:19)And the people said unto me, wilt thou not make known to us what those things are to us which thou hast done. (20)Then I said unto them, the word of Yahweh came unto me saying, (21)Speak to the house of Israel, thus saith the Lord Yahweh, Behold I will profane my sanctuary, the pride of thy strength, the desire of thine eyes and the compassion of thy souls, and thy sons and daughters which ye left shall fall by the sword. (22)And ye shall do as I have done, ye shall not cover thy lips and ye shall not eat the bread of men. (23)Thy tires shall be on thy heads and thy sandals on thy feet, and ye shall neither mourn nor weep but ye shall pine away in thine iniquities and one man shall moan over his brother. . .
> (25)And thou, son of man, shall it not be in that day when I will take from them their strength, the joy of their glory, the desire of their eyes and the lifting up of their soul, their sons and their daughters, (26)that in that day he who escaped may come to thee to make thine

ears hear. (27)In that day thy mouth will be opened to him who escaped and thou shalt speak and not be dumb any more, so thou shall be a sign unto them and they shall know that I am Yahweh.

(33:21)And it came to pass in the twelfth year of our captivity, in the tenth (month), in the fifth (day) of the month, that one who had escaped from Jerusalem came unto me saying, the city is smitten. (22)Now the hand of Yahweh had been upon me in the evening prior to the coming of the one who had escaped, and he opened my mouth until he came to me in the morning and my mouth was opened and I was not dumb any more.

(24:24)Thus shall Ezekiel be unto thee a sign; according to all that he hath done shall ye do: when this cometh, then ye shall know that I am Yahweh.

How can we possibly explain this general disorder in the latter part of chapter 24? It is probable that chapters 1-24 were the original written record of Ezekiel's prophecy and that the foreign-nations chapters are an appendix. Both sections are probably written down in the thirtieth year. Originally 33:21-22 was in the position to which we have shifted it above. The reason for the displacement will be discussed in connection with our general examination of chapter 33 as a whole.

But what of the position of verse 24? If it belongs at the end of the chapter, why has it been removed to its present position? Possibly this came about when 33:21-22 was removed, thus placing verses 27 and 24 one after the other. In both verses it is stated, once in the second person and once in the third person, that Ezekiel was to be a מופת to the people. When the editor saw that by removing two verses he had thrown together two others, and the second repeated the first, some alteration was definitely in order. Rather than delete a verse the editor moved it up to the end of the section interpreting the prophet's actions, where it seemed to be more naturally placed. This, we maintain, is the probable way by which the present disarrangement came about. Having said all this, we do not insist upon the removal of 24:24 from its present position, but the return of 33:21-22 to the end of chapter 24 is a very proper and necessary rearrangement. Ez. 24:24, whether or not we change its position, is the subscription to the original book of Ezekiel. If it remains in its present position, then verses 25-27 and 33:21-22 are but an account of the fulfilment of the predictions made in earlier oracles.

Chapters 1-24 constitute the original book of the prophet

and the foreign-nations section (Ez. 25-32) is an appendix. Although no final decision can be reached about the last nine chapters of the book, it is our tentative judgment that they existed independently and were written down soon after the vision. This conclusion rests on several observations: (a) These chapters contain exactly the sort of material which one would expect from a prophet-priest in the time of the Babylonian Exile. (b) There is nothing in the language which would point to a Hellenistic date (see Chapter III). (c) The psychological moment for such a vision would be the anniversary of the Temple's destruction. We doubt that this point would have occurred to a novelist, nor is it likely that it came about by accident.[31] (d) Our reconstruction of the East Gate (see Chapter II) leaves little room for doubt that the traditional date for these chapters is correct. (e) They were immediately recorded because the visionary recognised the importance of the details of a future restored temple in the homeland. Chapters 40 through 48 very probably circulated independently in written and oral form for some time before they were attached to the book itself.[32]

Before turning to chapters 33-39, which are the basic problem in any consideration of the composition, we should look a little more closely at the prophecy in the light of what has been said thus far. Ezekiel's book, as it now stands, is constructed on a rather interesting combination of a chronological framework with a secondary grouping according to subject matter. Each date in the prophecy marks an event either of tremendous personal or national significance. Imagine an old prophet reviewing his oracles with a group of disciples as an audience. While he spoke, it is probable that one of his followers took notes supplemented later from memory. There is good precedent for such "a secretary to the prophet" in Baruch, who recorded Jeremiah's utterances.[33] Ezekiel's memory reaches back across a quarter of a century to the fifth year (chapters 1-3) when he saw his vision of Yahweh and was commissioned as a prophet. The memory of the call was closely associated in his aging mind with the first vision (chapters 4-5) and his first major oracles (chapters 6-7). All these recollections clustered around his call as particles of metal are drawn to a magnet.

The next great event in the life of the prophet was his visionary return to Jerusalem (chapters 8-11), where he beheld the great religious iniquity and corruption which plagued his native land. Taking the vision as a starting point, Ezekiel continues to review in memory oracles which he had spoken regarding the corruptness of the land, the people, the kings, the priests and prophets. We do not for a moment believe that Ezekiel delivered these oracles on any one given date. They are contained in chapters 12 through 19 and must be considered undated matter. These oracles are placed here because their subject matter is directly related to the vision which the prophet saw (chapters 8-11). Most probably chapters 12 through 19 represent sermons which Ezekiel preached prior to the destruction of Jerusalem.

Another high point in the life of Ezekiel was the visit paid him by the elders of Israel (chapter 20), a visit which gave rise to a terrible oracle against the land and its leaders. In the thirtieth year the prophet included all his oracles on this subject which now make up chapters 21 through 23. Finally, chapter 24 becomes the real climax when the city's siege was begun and when Ezekiel's wife died.

It was, we think, in some way such as the foregoing that Ezekiel had chapters 1-24 arranged and written down in the thirtieth year of the captivity of Jehoiachin. These chapters were recorded by a scribe whose native tongue may still have been Hebrew but who also had a professional command of Aramaic. Had Ezekiel himself written the book we might expect less Aramaic, but the presence of loan words and morphological Aramaisms would be anticipated from a scribe who had spent all his adult life, or perhaps all his life, among Aramaic-speaking peoples (see Chapter III). Although we prefer this explanation, a second line of inference is possible in the light of the facts. Ezekiel could have spoken these to his disciples in "the thirtieth year" without any written record. After a few years of oral transmission, perhaps after the master's death, a record was put together. Either type of explanation is possible, and the evidence narrows the field down to a solution similar to one or the other.

One problem has long kept some students from accepting Ez. 1-24 as a unit; that is, the presence of the doublet in chapter 10 on the inaugural vision in chapter 1. Here we have actually nothing more than a repetition of an earlier vision. A second shorter repetition is recorded in 43:1-5. Chapters 8 through 11 appear to be the account of a single vision, as the text plainly states. Within these chapters there is an appropriate time and place for the Almighty to reappear. What form would Yahweh take in Ezekiel's mind? Of course, the answer is quite apparent. The Divine Being would appear in substantially the same form as He did in His initial appearance. This chapter is not a literary doublet; it is a second appearance of Yahweh to His prophet.

With this last obstacle gone, there remains no solid reason

for refusing to accept the first twenty-four chapters as the unit of a prophecy published by Ezekiel in the thirtieth year. These chapters are recorded in a combined chronological-topical scheme as described above.[34]

But what of the foreign-nations chapters? They were written down as an appendix to chapters 1-24, probably also in the thirtieth year. What bitterness must have welled up within the soul of the prophet when he remembered the way Judah's neighbors had acted when Jerusalem was being besieged! Is it any wonder that his oracles against these neighbors follow immediately the fall of Jerusalem? Nothing could be more natural! Of course little need be said about the dates in the Tyre (26-28) and Egypt (29-32) chapters. One interesting and disturbing date is the "twenty-seventh year" in 29:17. This date interrupts an oracle against Egypt in which dire consequences are being predicted. Suddenly the "twenty-seventh year" appears in the midst of the oracle. While talking about Egypt, the old prophet remembered a word which came to him regarding the land. The attack against Tyre had brought "no wages" to Nebuchadrezzar; for recompense, however, the booty from the Egyptian campaign would be all the greater. Here we see a normal association of ideas in the mind of a man who remembered past events from his long life.[35]

Such is our explanation of Ez. 1-24 and 25-32. It is a hypothesis which settles most of the problems and seems to fit in well with the book as it now stands. We have shown already how it explains the order of presentation, the presence of "the doublet" in chapter 10 and the "twenty-seventh year" in 29:17. Our view about the composition would also clear up the Pelatiah incident (11:13). While Ezekiel, standing in Babylon, uttered fearful denunciations against Pelatiah and others, Pelatiah died. This has always been a cardinal point in any argument about residence. Actually the verse is an interruption in the chapter and was probably inserted by Ezekiel when the book was recorded in the thirtieth year. The news of Pelatiah's death had reached the prophet's ears soon after Ezekiel had his vision of a visit to Jerusalem. hence in memory the two were joined.

So much for the first thirty-two chapters. What can be said about 33 through 39? A close examination of chapter 33 reveals that it consists of three doublets, a misplaced date and a popular tradition. When verses 21-22 are removed to their proper place at the end of chapter 24, there remain three doublets and a tradition about the eloquence of the prophet (33:20-33). The first section, vss. 1-9, seems beyond question to be a doublet of the "watchman" passage in 3:9-21. Just as clearly are vss. 10-20 a remarkable doublet of chapter 18. We cannot be as sure regarding 23-29, but it too looks like an inexact doublet of 11:14-21. At least, it is dealing with the same subject matter in almost the same way. Admittedly, anyone of these doublets could be prophetic variants on the same theme, but the case for doublets in chapter 33 is extremely strong. There remains nothing but the rather interesting tradition about the effect of Ezekiel's eloquence on the gôlāh (33:30-33).

Chapter 33 is the literary device with which a disciple of the great prophet was able to connect chapters 34 through 39 to the original book (chapters 1-32). What better literary binder could one seek than three excerpts from Ezekiel's oracles together with a popular tradition about the prophet himself? In trying to cover up the "late addition" this disciple-editor left literary finger-prints everywhere. Clumsily he transposed a date (vss. 21-22) from chapter 24 and put it in the middle of chapter 33, where it has absolutely no connection. Such a conglomeration could hardly be explained satisfactorily otherwise.

Finally, the disciple-editor or editors collected from memory or perhaps from written sources a splendid oracle on the shepherds of Israel (34), a bitter denunciation of Edom (35), a beautiful promise of restoration for Israel which is opposite to the theme of Ezekiel 6 (36) and the account of Ezekiel's vision of the valley of dry bones (37). None of these passages is dated, but they can probably be placed toward the end of the prophet's ministry, possibly even after "the thirtieth year." Exact dating of any of the material contained in these chapters is, we confess, impossible. It should be remembered that these oracles, even though added to the record by a later hand, originated with Ezekiel and are not secondary in the usual sense of the term. Possibly they were transmitted for a short time orally, but this is not at all certain. We presume that chapters 38 and 39, the enigmatic Gog and Magog section, also came from Ezekiel late in his prophetic career. There is no evidence to the contrary. In his day, as in later times, there was increasing menace from the north, and such a threat to security would necessarily have to be faced by a restored Israel.[36] The northern terror, Gog and Magog, would be overcome by Yahweh with finality, as described in this passage. Although many scholars deny the Gog and Magog section to our prophet and place it in the Persian period or later, we see no reason why these strange chapters could not have come from the mind of a man who lived among the Babylonian gôlāh.

Briefly, therefore, the book bearing the name Ezekiel can be ascribed in the main to Ezekiel, the traditional author. He did not write the book; that was done by one of his disciples in "the thirtieth year." Either as the prophet recalled the high points of his ministry or soon thereafter, the scribal-disciple made a record. In that "thirtieth year" the first twenty-four chapters became the original written book of Ezekiel's oracles of denunciation against Jerusalem and to these chapters were added the foreign-nations section as an appendix. Later, after the prophet's death, another editor-disciple collected neglected prophecies of his master (34-39), and added them to the original book. They were bound in by the use of chapter 33, which is made up of doublets on well-known oracles of Ezekiel. At the same time chapters 40 through 48, which had circulated independently, were added to complete the work. In this way Ezekiel's book took substantially its present form.

We admit that there may have been later additions and emendations to the book after it was put together. Nevertheless, the prophecy as a whole must be attributed to Ezekiel, the prophet of the Babylonian gôlāh. Two or more disciples are credited with the written form, but the source of the prophecy is to be traced directly to Ezekiel himself.

CONCLUSION

EZEKIEL was, as tradition always maintained, a prophet of the sixth century B.C. who was carried into captivity with many of his fellow countrymen by Nebuchadrezzar in 598 B.C. It was in Babylonia at a place called Tel-Abib that he saw his inaugural vision and received the call to be a prophet of Yahweh. His entire ministry was spent in Babylonia, and he never returned to his native land; however, in visionary experiences he often saw the familiar scenes and common occurrences of the Jerusalem area.

Objections to this point of view are without adequate foundation and rest mainly on the belief that a prophet must face his audience directly, else he is not truly a prophet. Once we realize that the prophet was capable of speaking to an unseen audience and that he never spoke to more than a small percentage of his intended audience, the whole argument against Babylonian locale loses its force. Besides this, the variant views about residence raise many more questions than they can settle, and the Babylonian view fits the facts better than any other explanation. Little things like the use of לִבְנָה, the mud-brick walls, the confused geography of Palestine and many other small but important facts add strong support to the traditional view.

Our prophet lived, not in the time of Manasseh, but in the time which tradition assigns him, that is, during the Babylonian Exile (598-539 B.C.). Upon examination the "late language" of Ezekiel evaporates, as does the "anachronism" of the references to Persians, to Daniel and to late religious rites. The Persians were already on the scene; Dan'el was a hero of the remote past like Job and Noah, not a contemporary of Ezekiel in the gôlāh; and the late religious rites are based on a confused, cryptic reference. Thanks to linguistic data, the records of Tyre which give us dates and the reconstruction of the East Gate, we can now be certain that Ezekiel was among the gôlāh and began to prophesy in 593 B.C., continuing his ministry until 570 B.C. or probably 567 B.C. when his book was published.

The Aramaic of the prophecy bearing Ezekiel's name is not nearly so extensive as scholars have led us to think. There are some loan-words, a larger number of Aramaized forms, but there is no sure trace of Aramaic syntax anywhere in the entire book. We know that Aramaic was the lingua franca of the ancient Near East in the sixth century B.C. Besides this we should expect to find some linguistic influence from Babylonia, where Aramaic was both the popular and official language. Even so, the influence came mainly from scribes whose native tongue was Hebrew but who had learned Aramaic, either since coming to Babylonia or if under their middle thirties, from infancy.

Contrary to a growing belief, Ezekiel was not a schizophrenic, nor is he to be classed as a psychopathic case of any kind. On the other hand, he would not fit the mould of normality even in his day. Therein lies his greatness; he was a sensitive spirit who was caught up in the cross currents of history. Torn from his native land and transplanted to a strange place, he turned inward and became perhaps the outstanding visionary of the Old Testament. Our prophet may correctly be classed with the world's best known mystics, but he did not deviate enough from normal to be called psychopathic. His ability to return to a normal role, apparently at will, undermines the diagnosis of schizophrenia which has so often been pinned on him.

It is unnecessary to attribute to Ezekiel the power of clairvoyance, as some have claimed. Many of his visions were general recollections of people and events which he had formerly seen; that is, his subconscious used previous conscious experiences as the material for visions. The words of Ezekiel do not describe an event which occurs simultaneously with his words; on the contrary, his oracles are about general trends and the specific occurrences described are probably typical in character.

In the thirtieth year of Jehoiachin's captivity Ezekiel dictated from memory the account of the oracles which he had delivered and the visions which he had seen during the years prior to the destruction of Jerusalem. The first twenty-four chapters of the present prophecy constitute the original book with the foreign-nations section being an appendix. This dictation was either remembered or taken down by one or more of Ezekiel's disciples who knew Aramaic as well as Hebrew. If the original book was recorded by memory in the thirtieth year, it most certainly was written down very soon thereafter. Chapters 1 through 24 are arranged on the framework of a chronological sequence of outstanding events with a secondary arrangement according to subject matter. The same is true of Ez. 25-32.

Later, probably after the death of the prophet himself, one or more disciples made a collection of Ezekiel's teachings. Naturally he started with the written work, chapters 1 through 32, and then gathered other material from memory and records. How could a disciple combine the two? By joining three doublets and moving the last two verses of chapter 24 (i.e., 33:21-22) he was able to create a literary binder in the form of chapter 33. Thus he united his independent material with the original book and also attached chapters 40-48, a well-known vision of the prophet, to the collection.

The traditional view of Ezekiel is substantially correct throughout. He was the prophet of the Babylonian gôlāh, among whom all his ministry was spent (593-567 B.C.). A great mystic, he was also a practical leader of men who merits the title: Father of Post-exilic Judaism. The book which bears his name is largely the product of his mind, even though written down, in part at least, by others. His dominant purpose was "that ye may know that I am the Lord Yahweh," and his consuming passion was the vindication of Yahweh. In all, Ezekiel was one of the greatest spiritual figures of ancient Israel.

FOOTNOTES

Introduction

1. Cf. G.F. Moore, Judaism, Cambridge, 1947, Vol.I, pp. 246-47, 300.
2. Cf. Shalom Spiegel, HTR, XXIV, 1931, p. 245.
3. John Calvin wrote three volumes on the first thirteen chapters of Ezekiel but never finished the commentary for reasons which elude us.
4. The figures of Gog and Magog were brought over into the New Testament by the author of the book of Revelation (cf. Rev. 20:7-10). In this case the two kings and their armies represent the very epitome of evil which will be overcome at the end of the Age. Growing out of Revelation and Ezekiel 38-39 has come the popular belief in a last battle which is called the battle of Armegeddon. One cannot be at all certain what threatening forces Ezekiel originally had in mind since the passing years and fanciful interpretations have obscured his original intent.
5. Shalom Spiegel, op. cit., p. 247.
6. Ibid., p. 248.
7. Ibid., p. 250-51.
8. Ez. 4:4-8 pictures the prophet as lying on one side 390 days in order to bear the iniquity of Israel and 40 days to bear the iniquity of Judah. Each day of his being in this odd position represents a year in the history of the respective countries. By adding these two figures and subtracting them from 593 B.C. (Ezekiel's call) Soinecke arrives at the date 163 B.C., but the reason for his deciding that the time element refers to subsequent history is beyond us. His whole theory is extremely ridiculous and rests on the violation of all accepted grammatical and historical rules of objective research.
9. J.E. McFadyen, Introduction to the Old Testament, New York, 1933, p. 162.
10. Gustav Hölscher's Hezekiel, der Dichter und das Buch appeared in 1924, and C.C. Torrey published Pseudo-Ezekiel and the Original Prophecy in 1931; therefore McFadyen had either failed to keep up or discounted these efforts as of no importance.
11. S.R. Driver, Introduction to the Literature of the Old Testament, Edinburgh, 1913, p. 279.
12. R. Kraetzschmar (Ezechiel, Handkommentar des Alten Testaments, Gottingen, 1900) was greatly impressed by the doublets in the prophecy and was the first to propose a two-recension theory; one in the first person and the other in the third person. Herrmann (Ezechielstudien, Leipzig, 1908; Ezechiel in

Sellin's Kommentar, Leipzig, 1924) believed that the various oracles or recensions were redacted by none other than the prophet himself in Babylon.

13. Gustav Hölscher decided that the genuine parts of Ezekiel are written in a definite poetic metre, or at least that is what can be attributed to Ezekiel with certainty. With this as a criterion Hölscher proceeded to cut the text down until there were less than 175 verses remaining in whole or in part which he admits as true Ezekiel, (cf. Hezekiel, der Dichter und das Buch, Beihefte ZAW, 1924).

14. Since the time of Wellhausen critical scholars have depended upon Ezekiel as a datable book by which the Priestly material (i.e., P) in the Pentateuch could be accurately pegged chronologically. The date of Ezekiel was in their minds absolutely fixed. Since the prophet of the Exile at times shows definite affinities with the Priestly mind as reflected especially in Leviticus 17-26, the so-called Holiness Code, it was perfectly safe to date the Priestly stratum of the Pentateuch about 550 B.C. Of course a confusion would result in the Biblical literary chronology of scholars who approach the Old Testament from a strictly Wellhausenian point of view if Ezekiel's date is altered.

Chapter I

1. Cf. W.F. Albright, From the Stone Age to Christianity, Baltimore, 1940, pp. 246-250; G.A. Cooke, Ezekiel in ICC, New York, 1937, pp. xx-xxvii; Rudolph Kittel, Geschichte des Volkes Israel, III, Stuttgart, 1927, pp. 144-150; Adolphe Lods, The Prophets and the Rise of Judaism, New York, 1937, pp. 173-180; Otto Eissfeldt, Einleitung in das Alte Testament, Tubingen, 1934, pp. 411ff.; J.E. McFadyen, Introduction to the Old Testament, pp. 162ff.; Ernst Sellin, Introduction to the Old Testament, London, 1923, pp. 152-56; Joseph Ziegler, Echter Bibel, Ezechiel, Würzburg, 1948, p. 6.

2. Cf. W.O.E. Oesterley and T.H. Robinson, Introduction to the Books of the Old Testament, New York, 1937, p. 319.

3. Cf. P. Auvray, "Le Problème Historique du Livre d'Ezechiel," Revue Biblique, LV, 1948, pp. 509-10.

4. This eight-point summary was taken from W.H. Brownlee's unpublished Master's thesis, Major Critical Problems of the Book of Ezekiel but has been expanded from other sources. Cf. Oesterley and Robinson, Introduction, pp. 318-19; I.G. Matthews, Ezekiel, An American Commentary on the Old Testament, Philadelphia, 1939, pp. vii-ix; E.L. Allen, Prophet and Nation, London, 1947, pp. 95-102; P. Auvray, Revue Biblique, LV, 1948, pp. 503 ff. et al.

5. Cf. Volkmar Herntrich, Ezechielprobleme, Beihefte ZAW, LXI,

Giessen, 1932, pp. 73-130.
6. I.G. Matthews, op. cit., pp. xvii-xviii.
7. Ibid., pp. xviii-xxiii.
8. Cf. J. Battersby Harford, Studies in the Book of Ezekiel, Cambridge, 1935, pp. 77-101.
9. Cf. Alfred Bertholet, Hesekiel, Handbuch zum Alten Testament, Tübingen, 1936, pp. xxiii-xix.
10. P. Auvray, op. cit., pp. 503-519.
11. A. Van den Born, "De Historische Situatie van Ezechiels Prophetie," Ephemerides theologicae Lovanienses, XXIII, 1947, pp. 1-27.
12. O.R. Fisher's The Unity of the Book of Ezekiel was not available for first hand study, but R.H. Pfeiffer, under whom this doctoral dissertation was written, has given a summary in his Introduction to the Old Testament, New York, 1941, p. 531.
13. D.N. Freedman wrote The Theology of Ezekiel while at Princeton Seminary and has given some of the positions held at the time (cf. pp. 86-124).
14. Oesterley and Robinson, op. cit., pp. 328-29.
15. Cf. C.C. Torrey, Pseudo-Ezekiel and the Original Prophecy, pp. 24-44.
16. Cf. James Smith, The Book of the Prophet Ezekiel, London, 1931, pp. 15-21.
17. Ibid., pp. 55-71.
18. Ibid.
19. G.A. Danell, Studies in the Name Israel in the Old Testament, Upsala, 1946, pp. 254-55.
20. Our prophet, like Jeremiah (Jer. 24), pins all his hopes for revival of the nation on the captives in Babylon, who will be the purged righteous nucleus for a future nation under God. In two bitter exchanges between the Exiles and those Jews still living in Jerusalem Ezekiel left no doubt that his feelings were for the members of the gôlāh (cf. 11:14-21; 33:24-29).
21. Besides Jeremiah's letter, which seems to have reached Babylon unhindered, there is the fact that a fugitive from the smitten city was able to make his way to Tel-Abib (33:31-22). Jeremiah's interest in those Jews who had been carried into captivity also lends credence to the fact that Ezekiel had a dual interest in the two segments of Israel. Caravans were constantly plying their way between Palestine and Mesopotamia carrying not only goods but detailed news of events in both places.
22. Cf. G.A. Cooke, op. cit., p. xxiv.
23. A friend has just related to me how Austrian prisoners of World War II, taken during the fighting on the Eastern Front, played games in which they made transfers from regular streetcar routes in Vienna. These prisoners were being held captive in Siberia. We are all aware of the intense interest which American Jews have shown in events at modern Tel Aviv during the

last few months. This amazing interest came from people who have no desire to return to Israel but feel a kinship to the land and the people. Also pertinent to this discussion would be the interest shown by refugees from Russia after 1917 and Germany after 1933 in their homelands, even though separated from them.

24. Cf. discussion below.

25. Cf. Danell, op. cit., pp. 245f.

26. Pharaoh Necho made a desperate attempt to stem the Chaldean tide by going to the aid of the weak Assyrian forces. On his way North the Egyptian leader either executed or killed Josiah in open battle (609 B.C.) when the Jewish king opposed the march through Palestine (II Kgs. 23:28-30). The death of the king gave the populace in Jerusalem opportunity to express their feeling in supporting Jehoahaz for the throne (II Kgs.23: 30), but during the ascendency of Egyptian influence Jehoahaz was dethroned and Jehoiakim became a good vassal of Egypt (II Kgs. 23:31-36). In 605 B.C. the battle of Carchemish brought complete defeat of Egyptian forces, who were put to rout and pursued by Nebuchadrezzar to the border of Egypt itself. Jehoiakim immediately shifted allegiance to Babylon and remained apparently loyal for three years, after which he rebelled. When attacks by Syrians, Moabites and other neighboring peoples failed to bring the desired results, Nebuchadrezzar took over the campaign which ended in surrender by Jehoiachin, who had succeeded to the throne after the death of Jehoiakim, which occurred during the siege (II Kgs. 24:1-9). Leading citizens of the Jewish community in Judah were taken to Babylon, and Zedekiah (Mattaniah) was put on the throne by the Chaldeans. In the course of his reign there were two strong factions in Jerusalem. One urged submission to Babylon and the other wanted to rebel with the promised aid of Egypt. Jeremiah favored submission to Babylon because he believed Nebuchadrezzar to be the servant of Yahweh (Jer. 25:9b; 27:6). Ezekiel felt that Zedekiah in breaking his oath of loyalty to the Babylonian king was worthy of nothing better than destruction (Ez. 17:11-21). In spite of the protestations of the prophets the Egyptian party won the day and revolt against Babylon began in the ninth year of Zedekiah's reign. During the siege Egypt under Pharaoh Hophra made one vain attempt to rescue the besieged city (Jer. 37:1-5). This whole struggle between pro-Egyptian and pro-Babylonian forces, even though its focal point was in Palestine, must have been followed closely at Tel-Abib.

27. The two proverbs to which we have reference are those found in 12:21-28. In substance the people are guilty of wishful thinking in both cases. First, they convince themselves that the prophet's predictions of destruction will not be fulfilled and then decide that these terrible events will not

occur in their time. Thinking of this kind would be common to the optimists among any city under siege.

28. Cf. above.

29. Many more maps are known: B. Meissner, Babylonien und Assyrien, II, Heidelberg, 1920-25, pp. 377f. Note also the plans of Nippur and its environs (H.V. Hilprecht, Explorations in Bible Lands during the Nineteenth Century, Philadelphia, 1903, p. 518), and half a dozen other maps, all from Neo-Babylonian times. Much earlier is the Nuzi map from the twenty-third and twenty-second century B.C. (BASOR 48, 3; T. Meek, Excavations at Nuzi, III, Cambridge, 1935, p. xvii).

30. Cf. James L. Kelso, The Ceramic Vocabulary of the Old Testament, New Haven, 1948, pp. 36-37.

31. It would be very remarkable if a Babylonian redactor were able to add subtle touches such as the mud brick walls and the נְכֹה plus the relative usage of Israel and Judah. Those who believe that a redactor actually changed the scene of the book have never explained this phenomenon, but rather blame only those passages in which reference is directly made to a Babylonian setting on this late writer (Auvray, op. cit., p. 509).

32. Rudolph Kittel, op. cit., p. 146.

33. When an author seeks in one or more redactors the answer to minor literary difficulties, he makes it likely that eventually his reconstruction will become almost completely subjective. The dangers of this method can hardly be overemphasized.

34. Herntrich, op. cit., p. 130.

35. Ibid., pp. 126-27.

36. G.A. Cooke, op. cit., p. xxiv.

37. Ezekiel's philosophy of history simply stated was: Rebellion against Yahweh will bring destruction upon the guilty parties.

38. The marvelous descriptions of Tyre and Egypt lead Matthews to think that the prophet had a first-hand knowledge of these places.

39. Cf. J.B. Harford, op. cit.

40. If we change the date of Ez. 33:21 to the eleventh year instead of the twelfth, which is a necessary correction, that still means over five months were required to bring the news from Jerusalem (cf. II Kgs. 25:3, Jer. 39:2; 52:6). We should expect the tragic news of a disaster like the Fall of the Jewish capital to spread through Judah almost instantaneously.

41. The text of Ezekiel clearly marks the action of removal as symbolic and not real. This fact plus the time which elapsed between the Fall of Jerusalem and the news of that event's reaching the prophet leaves this part of Bertholet's residence-theory without support.

42. P. Auvray, op. cit., p. 516.

43. A. Bertholet, op. cit., p. xvi.

44. Fisher's view makes our prophet active in Jerusalem for six years prior to the Fall. It is hardly conceivable that he could have escaped Chaldean notice for such a length of time.
45. Oesterley and Robinson, op. cit., pp. 328-29.
46. This argument is completely invalid since by it the failure of one contemporary to mention another in extant writings would be taken as an indication that the unmentioned person was fictional. Hosea does not take note of Amos, nor does Nehemiah refer to Ezra, and so the list could be extended.
47. The tradition reflected in Daniel would lead one to conclude that the Chaldeans required religious obedience from their vassals. However that may be, the policy probably vacillated between extreme strictness and laxity of enforcement. The Persians were the first to practice something akin to religious toleration; before that time political supremacy meant religious conformity to the victor's religion.
48. Cf. I.G. Matthews, op. cit., p. xxi; Shalom Spiegel, HTR. XXIV, 1931, p. 273.
49. We cannot be sure either about the extent or nature of the idolatry current in Judah at this time, but it undoubtedly had features common with that which once held sway in North Israel.
50. Herntrich, op. cit., p. 128.
51. W.F. Albright, "The Seal of Eliakim," JBL, LI, 1932, pp. 100-101.

Chapter II

1. Cf. R.H. Pfeiffer, op. cit., pp. 527-28.
2. Ibid., p. 528.
3. C.C. Torrey, Pseudo-Ezekiel, pp. 102-113.
4. Ibid., pp. 15-23.
5. Ibid., pp. 31-33.
6. Ibid., p. 57.
7. Ibid., pp. 46ff.
8. Ibid., pp. 69-70.
9. Ibid., p. 84. After reading Spiegel's discussion regarding this strange rite and looking at Torrey's answer, it is our conclusion that the brief description of the rite is entirely too cryptic to allow for an accurate identification with a definite cultic rite of any age. For a thoroughgoing discussion see S. Spiegel, HTR, XXIV, 1931, pp. 298-301 and C.C. Torrey, "Certainly Pseudo-Ezekiel," JBL, LIII, 1934, pp. 302-306.
10. Ibid., pp. 84-93.
11. Ibid., pp. 98-99.
12. James Smith, op. cit., pp. 90-100.
13. Cf. Nils Messel, Ezechielfragen, Oslo, 1945, pp. 21-25.
14. C.C. Torrey, "Ezekiel and the Exile, A Reply," JBL, LI, 1932, pp. 179-181.

15. C.C. Torrey, Second Isaiah, New York, 1928, p. 29.
16. Ibid., p. 62.
17. W.F. Albright, "The American Excavations at Tell Beit Mirsim," ZAW, VI, 1929, p. 16.
18. S. Spiegel, HTR, 1932, p. 262.
19. Ibid., pp. 258-59.
20. Ibid., pp. 260-61.
21. Ibid., pp. 281f.
22. C.C. Torrey, Pseudo-Ezekiel, pp. 21-22.
23. Talmud, Baba Bathra, 15a.
24. See above for discussion.
25. C.C. Torrey, op. cit., pp. 48-57.
26. S. Spiegel, op. cit., p. 314.
27. In one of these tablets which Weidner has published we have listed one Mede, but four Persians, which would certainly indicate that Persians were already on the historical scene (cf. Mélanges syriens offerts à Monsieur René Dussaud, p. 930). Added to this is the fact we have the inscription of Ariaramnes, the great uncle of Cyrus the Elder, in which he assumes the title "King of Kings." Further we now have a text from the time of Assurbanapli in which mention is made of an embassy sent to Cyrus, king of Persia, in 639 B.C. Though Persia was not an empire like Media at such an early date, she had become a most important state at least two generations before the name appears in Ezekiel's prophecies (cf. W.F. Albright, JBL, LI, 1932, pp. 98-99).
28. The difference in spelling between the Biblical Daniel and Ugaritic Dan'el would not be conclusive except for the support received from the fact that Daniel of the Babylonian gôlāh would be completely out of place in the company of such ancient figures as Noah and Job. Furthermore it should be pointed out that Danel, the father of Enoch's wife Edni, appears in the book of Jubilees 4:20, probably from the third century B.C. Here again the spelling is the same as the Ras Shamra Dan'el.
29. Chapter III deals with the Aramaic question.
30. Burrows lists under Exilic and post-Exilic material the Song of Moses (Deut. 32) along with I and II Kgs. and many other passages which scholarship now dates as preëxilic. Certainly the literary sources of Kings existed long before the Exile. The Song of Moses, in the light of Ras Shamra discoveries, proves to be very early. Dependence upon such passages or their sources would hardly point to an extremely late date for the prophecy. Regarding the so-called borrowing of Ezekiel from admittedly late material, one would do well to remember that the borrowing could easily have been by these late sources from Ezekiel. In the case of Ezra-Nehemiah-Chronicles data in the book, if there be such it most probably came from the ancient sources of this work. What was considered late material in 1925

has proved in many cases to be quite ancient (cf. Millar Burrows, The Literary Relations of Ezekiel, New Haven, 1925, pp. 19ff.).

31. James Smith, op. cit., pp. 19-20.
32. See discussion above.
33. C.C. Torrey, op. cit., p. 60.
34. Ibid., p. 61.
35. James Smith, op. cit., p. 94.
36. Ibid., pp. 94-95.
37. Ibid., p. 95.
38. Ibid., pp. 98-99.
39. Ibid., p. 99.
40. W.A. Irwin, The Problem of Ezekiel, Chicago, 1943, pp. 263-65.
41. Ibid., p. 266.
42. Ibid., p.265.
43. Ibid., p. 268.
44. G.R. Berry, "The Composition of the Book of Ezekiel," JBL, 1939, pp. 163-175.
45. Cf. Hugo Gressmann, Altorientalische Texte zum Alten Testament, Berlin and Leipzig, 1926, pp. 46-49.
46. I.G. Matthews, op. cit., pp. xxi-xviii.
47. W.F. Albright, JBL, 1932, p. 96.
48. Cf. Louis Finkelstein, The Pharisees, Philadelphia, 1938, pp. 632-33.
49. Ibid., also see above.
50. See earlier discussion.
51. G.A. Cooke, op. cit., p. 4.
52. Norman H. Snaith, "The Dates in Ezekiel," Expository Times, 1948, pp. 315-16.
53. Ibid., p. 316.
54. Ibid.
55. Snaith's fanciful work, like many others, assumes that the dates in verses 1 and 2 must be synchronized, therefore he accepts this unheard of, unparalleled system of dating by the king's age. When one system does not fit all dates, he supplies a second. In all, this is one of the weakest explanations thus far advanced.
56. W.F. Albright, op. cit., p. 97; cf. S. Spiegel, HTR, 1932, pp. 282ff.
57. This important point has often been suggested by W.F. Albright. (Cf. JBL, LI, 1932, p. 93.
58. Weidner, Mélanges Dussaud, op. cit., pp. 925-26.
59. Otto Eissfeldt, "Das Datum der Belagerung von Tyrus durch Nebuchadnezar," FuF, 10, 1934, p. 165 (reprint).
60. Ibid., pp. 164f.
61. Ibid., p.168.
62. (Vs.5)We read "seven steps" with the Greek since that

number of steps is twice mentioned in connection with other
gates described in this chapter (40: 22, 26). καὶ διεμέτρησεν
is added by the LXX. (Vs.7) ויחל בין should be read on the
basis of the LXX. It is necessary to point out that αιλαμ used
in the LXX sometimes means "vestibule" but is often confused
with שילים meaning "piers." ἕξ in the LXX is a mistake for
πέντε . The long explanatory insertion, καὶ τὸ θεε τὸ δεύτερον
ἴσον τῷ καλάμῳ πλάτος καὶ ἴσον τῷ καλάμῳ μῆκος is
certainly not original. The LXX reading καὶ τὸ αἰλὰμ πήχεων
is most probably a misplaced measurement for one of the piers.
The meaning of the last part of the verse which is omitted in
the LXX is very obscure, but this obscurity probably arises
from our ignorance of the temple building not from a textual
mistake. The distance referred to in ואולם השער מאצל
השער מהבית קנה אחד must remain a mystery for the time
being. (Vss.8 and 9)In these verses מהבית קנה אחד וימד
את אלם השער is a perfectly obvious exact verti-
cal dittography from the above line and should be excised from
the text. καὶ τὸ θεε τὸ τρίτον ἴσον τῷ καλάμῳ πλάτος καὶ
ἴσον τῷ καλάμῳ μῆκος in LXX rendering of verses is evidently a later explanatory gloss with no place in the original
text. The last three words in the MT, ואולם השער מהבית though
supported by the LXX are probably to be explained as a dittography from the line above. (Vs.10)In a very corrupt text the
MT and LXX agree on the rendering of this verse. (Vs.11)The LXX
translator undoubtedly reads רחב where we have שער and so translated it with εὖρος which probably refers correctly to the overall measurement of the inner vestibule as over against the ten
cubit opening of the gate itself. (Vs.12)The LXX translator
probably took גבול to mean a place where people might gather
when passing traffic forced them from the main thoroughfare,
thus the translation ἐπισυναγόμενος . This, however, is by
no means certain. האחת is more probably read האחד. Greek and
Syriac read correctly for מפּה, מפּה הפּה. Apparently the
second אמה is the result of a horizontal dittography since
"one" in this case must modify הגבול , e.g., "one border on
this side and on that side." (Vs.13)The word גג definitely
seems to be out of place here especially since the LXX has
"wall." By emending גג to גד we arrive at the word which the
Greek translator possibly understood as "wall." Twenty-five
cubits is most probably the outside measurement for the breadth
of the gate structure. In our reconstruction of the gate, however, we have dotted in a second thickness for the wall, i.e.,
$4\frac{1}{2}$ cubits. This possibility is suggested by the thickness of
the Megiddo walls (Fig. 2) plus the fact that the walls in our
reconstruction seem rather flimsy (Fig.1). Admittedly certainty
cannot be hoped for in this matter. (Vs.14) ויעש cannot possibly be correct since the visionary figure was not constructing

anything but simply measuring a building already in existence. וַיָּמָד is a feasible correction in view of the constant usage of the verb in this whole passage. Verse 14 as it now stands makes no sense in the LXX or MT. We propose on the basis of both MT and LXX the following emended reading, וימד אילם השער מחוץ עשרים אמה ושש אמות איל החצר : אילים is the result of confusion with אולם and should be restored to אילו with the LXX. The emendation השער מחוץ is possibly correct here but without textual support. עשרים is read following the LXX. Then שׁשׁים should be read שׁשׁ followed by אמות since such a mistake could easily be explained by the carrying of the plural ending from the previous word. אֵיל is a dittography and איל is most probably a more correct rendering here. The exact meaning of החצר השער escapes us, but in general it means those piers closest to the court within the walls. סביב סביב is a vertical dittography from verse 16 where the expression occurs twice. By a composite reading of MT and LXX we are able at last to make some sense of the verse. Galling and Cooke are misled by the Greek εἴκοσι and propose an amazingly strange inner vestibule on the basis thereof (cf. Cooke, Ezekiel in the ICC, II, pp. 431ff. and Bertholet, Hesekiel in HZAT, pp. 137-138). Our emendation does away with the necessity for such unlikely proposals. (Vs.15) MT and LXX are in almost perfect accord. (Vs.16)Starting with the assumption that windows would hardly have been left in piers which were approximately thirteen feet thick, we propose that there has been some mixup between אל אלי המה on the one hand and אל איל תמרים. We presume therefore that the reference to the piers has nothing to do with windows but is a description of engaged pilasters, which were often found in temple construction. Our reconstruction would read: וחלנות אטמות אל התאים לפנימה לשער סביב סביב וכן לאלמנות לפנימה לשער סביב סביב ואל אילים תמרים.

63. In a private letter to W.F. Albright Von Soden mentioned this important observation which has not yet reached publication.

64. איל is possibly a popular etymology from "ram" to "battering ram" hence "pillar" or "jamb," because there would be a resemblance between a battering ram and these pillars. For further details see BASOR, 117, pp. 16f., note 7.

65. Cf. Megiddo II, Gordon Loud, Chicago, 1948, p. 48.

66. Carchemish, II, C.L. Woolley, The Town Defences, London, 1921, Plates 4 and 12.

Chapter III

1. Cf. F. Selle, De Aramaismis Libri Ezechielis, Halle,1890.
2. Cf. C.C. Torrey, Pseudo-Ezekiel, pp. 86-90; S. Spiegel, op. cit., pp. 302-303.

3. For a very good discussion of Aramean beginnings in the second millennium, cf. R.T. O'Callaghan, Aram Naharaim (Analecta Orientalia 26), Rome, 1948. Also see Raymond A. Bowman, "Arameans, Aramaic and the Bible," JNES, VII, pp. 65-90.

4. Cf. II Sam. 8:3-8; 10.

5. Cf. I Kgs. 11:23-25.

6. The account of the relations between these two states is found in the records of Kings and Chronicles. Once they combined forces at Qarqar (853 B.C.) and stemmed the Assyrian tide, but usually they were in conflict. War seemed to be the normal relationship between them from this time onward until Rezin and Pekah teamed up against Judah and doing so brought their own doom at the hands of Assyria (II Kgs. 16:5-9).

7. Cf. A. Bowman, "The Old Aramaic Alphabet at Tell Halaf," AJSL, LVIII, pp. 359-367, and Godfrey Driver, Semitic Writing, London, 1948, pp. 119-120.

8. Cf. W.F. Albright, "A Votive Stele Erected by Ben-Hadad I of Damascus to the God Melcarth," BASOR, 87, pp. 23-29, and G. Driver, op. cit., p. 120.

9. Cf. F. Thureau-Dangin, A. Barrois, G. Dossin and Maurice Dunand, Arslan Tash, Paris, 1931, pp. 136-37; Franz Rosenthal, Die aramaistische Forschung, Leiden, 1939, pp. 12-13 and G. Driver, op. cit., pp. 119-120.

10. Albright, op. cit., p. 25; Rosenthal, op. cit., pp. 9-10.

11. Cf. Rosenthal, pp. 6-8 and G. Driver, pp. 120-121.

12. Ibid., pp. 10-14.

13. "The influence of the Aramaic language has been out of all proportion to the political importance of the people who spoke it, for Aramaic soon became a cultural element at home almost everywhere in the ancient world." R.A. Bowman, JNES, VII, p. 66.

14. Cf. James H. Breasted, "The Physical Processes of Writing in the Early Orient," AJSL, XXXII, pp. 242-44. These are taken from Layard, Monuments of Assyria, I, 58; II, 36.

15. Cf. Louis Delaporte, Épigraphes Araméens, Paris, 1912, pp. 25-49; Bowman, op. cit., pp. 73f.; and G. Driver, op. cit. p. 122.

16. Bowman, op. cit., p. 74.

17. Cf. A. Cowley, Aramaic Papyri of the Fifth Century B.C., Oxford, 1923, p. xv.

18. Bowman, op. cit., p. 74.

19. Mark Lidzbarski, Altaramäische Urkunden aus Assur, Leipzig, 1921.

20. J. Friedrich et al, Die Inschriften vom Tell Halaf, (Archiv fur Orientforschung), Berlin, 1940, pp. 70-78.

21. Cf. M. Sprengling, "An Aramaic Seal Impression from Khorsabad," AJSL, XLIX, pp. 53-55.

22. II Kgs. 18:26-35; Is. 36:11-12.

23. "The names of places and persons involved in the letter, including the kings, are all Assyrian or Babylonian, and there are traces of Akkadian language and usage in vocabulary and syntax but the language in which it is written is definitely Aramaic." Bowman, op. cit., p. 76.

24. Cf. J. Payne Smith, A Compendious Syriac Dictionary, Oxford, 1903, p. 9; Mark Lidzbarski, Nordsemitische Epigraphik, Weimar, 1898, p. 210.

25. Cf. J.P. Smith, op. cit., p. 585; Muss-Arnolt, A Concise Dictionary of the Assyrian Language, Berlin, 1905, p. 767.

26. Cf. Muss-Arnolt, ibid., p. 360; R.P. Smith, Thesaurus Syriacus, p. 1567.

27. Cf. Cowley, op. cit., p. xv.

28. Cf. James A. Montgomery, The Book of Daniel, New York, 1927, p. 144; R.H. Charles, A Critical and Exegetical Commentary on the Book of Daniel, Oxford, 1929, pp. 29-30.

29. H.L. Ginsberg, "An Aramaic Contemporary of the Lachish Letters," BASOR, 111, pp. 24-27; John Bright, "A New Letter in Aramaic, Written to a Pharaoh in Egypt," Biblical Archeologist, XII, pp. 46-52.

30. Ibid., p. 24.

31. Henceforth in this paper the reference Selle refers to op. cit.

32. W.F. Albright in a forthcoming article.

33. B.G.= Carl Bezold and Albrecht Götze, Babylonisch-Assyrisches Glossar, Heidelberg, 1926.

34. M.A.= Muss-Arnolt, A Concise Dictionary of the Assyrian Language. Jast.= Marcus Jastrow, A Dictionary of the Targumim, The Talmud Babli and Yerushalmi and the Midrashic Literature, London, 1903. P.S.= Payne Smith, A Compendious Syriac Dictionary.

35. G.B.=W. Gesenius and F. Buhl, Hebräisches und Aramäisches Handwörterbuch über das Alte Testament, Leipzig, 1921.

36. Cf. Cyrus Gordon, Ugaritic Handbook, Rome, 1947, p. 232.

37. D. Luckenbill, The Annals of Sennacherib: "The Prism Inscription," Chicago, 1924, Col. III, line 42 on p. 34.

38. Every new Hebrew inscription seems to disclose one or more words which were previously unknown (e.g., Siloam Inscription, the Lachish ostraca).

39. Cf. H.C. Rawlinson, Miscellaneous Inscriptions of Assyria, London, 1866, II, p. 49, No. 3.

40. Cf. Z.S. Harris, A Grammar of the Phoenician Language, New Haven, 1936, p. 143.

41. Adolf Erman and Hermann Grapow, Wörterbuch der Aegyptischen Sprache, V, Leipzig, 1931, p. 207.

42. Cf. W.F. Albright, JAOS, 66, 1946, p. 318. Egyptian gif "monkey" is קוף and the place name Grg-pth becomes קרקפתה in Semitic. Cf. Godfrey Driver, op. cit., p. 86.

43. Gordon, op. cit., pp. 41-74.
44. Cf. G.A. Cooke, The Book of Ezekiel, pp. 26-27.
45. Cf. Emil Forrer, Die Provinzeinteilung des assyrischen Reiches, Leipzig, 1920, p. 115.
46. Cf. E. Kautzsch, Gesenius' Hebrew Grammar, Oxford, 1910, 67y.
47. Cf. W.F. Albright, BASOR, 94, p. 23, note 73.
48. Cooke, op. cit., pp. 294-95.
49. Torrey, Pseudo-Ezekiel, pp. 88-89.
50. Ibid., p. 90.
51. Space prohibits a complete discussion of the language of Chronicles, but a few illustrations of Aramaic influence should be pointed out. The Hebrew vocabulary is demonstrated by Curtis to be full of Aramaic loan words (cf. E.L. Curtis, The Books of Chronicles, New York, 1910, pp. 28-35).

Once ל is used for emphasis (I Ch. 29:6), and it is often found as a sign of the direct object (cf. I Ch. 16:37; 18:6; 25:1; 29:22, II Ch. 5:12; 6:42; 17:7, etc.). In other cases ל with the infinitive expresses tendency, intention or obligation (cf. I Ch. 6:34; 9:25; 10:13; 22:5; II Ch. 2:8; 8:13; 11:22, etc.). Of course, this construction is found in earlier language but not so extensively as is the case in later times.

The Chronicler no longer employs apposition for weight and measure as was the common Hebrew practice, and the general syntax of the numbers is like that of Biblical Aramaic.

Preference for waw copulative over waw consecutive, and the disappearance of ויהי points directly to Aramaizing. Along this same line subordinate, temporal and causal clauses are placed at the beginning of the sentence without being introduced by ויהי (e.g., I Ch. 21:15; II Ch. 5:13; 7:1; 12:7, 12, etc.).

Word order is different, usually having "subject-object-predicate" instead of the regular Hebrew order. There also seems to be a preference for the participle as over against the finite verb. Often בן replaces עשה, and there are many other Aramaisms in the book; however, these should suffice to show that the language of the Chronicles is much later than that of Ezekiel (cf. Arno Kropat, Die Syntax des Autors der Chronik, Beihefte ZAW, XVI, Giessen, 1909, especially pp. 72-75).

W.F. Albright summarized the linguistic picture as follows: "If Ezra was the Chronicler, many difficulties disappear. The incorporation of his memoirs in the first person, but in exactly the style and diction characteristic elsewhere of the Chronicler, becomes perfectly intelligible. The peculiar diction in question, which is saturated with Aramaisms, though it remains plastic and shows development in the direction of Mishnaic Hebrew, is perfectly in accord with Ezra's background. Since he came from at least four generations of Babylonian-born Jews, his Hebrew had become thoroughly Aramaized. Yet Ezra knew Hebrew; the Hebrew of the Chronicler is a living language," (W.F. Albright in a forthcoming article in the Marx Anniversary Volume).

The question as to whether Ezra was or was not the Chronicler does not concern us here. Be that as it may, the language of the book is in fact thoroughly Aramaized, exhibiting more than a century of linguistic development between it and Ezekiel's work.

52. Cf. C.C. Torrey, "The Question of the Original Language of Qoheleth," JQR, XXXIX, pp. 151-160.

Chapter IV

1. Maslow and Mittelmann list the following difficulties which arise in connection with an attempt to arrive at a "norm."
   1. Normality is always relative to the particular culture or subculture in which the person lives. 2. Normality is also relative to status, age, sex and type of personality. 3. It is difficult to separate the normative from the descriptive; that is, it is difficult to describe the personality objectively, without reference to values, ideals, or individual political or social beliefs. 4. There are many kinds of normality. 5. There is no clear line between the normal and the abnormal. 6. Much of what we know about the normal is obtained by extrapolation from the abnormal, and so may be inaccurate. (Maslow and Mittelmann, *Principles of Abnormal Psychology*, New York, 1941, pp. 37-38.

2. Cf. W.F. Albright, *From the Stone Age to Christianity*, pp. 248-49.
3. Edwin C. Broome, "Ezekiel's Abnormal Personality," JBL, 1946, pp. 277-292.
4. L.P. Thorpe and Barney Katz, *The Psychology of Abnormal Behavior*, New York, 1948, pp. 615-16.
5. Ibid., pp. 616-17.
6. Norman Cameron, *The Psychology of Behavior Disorders*, New York, 1947, pp. 468ff.
7. For complete discussions of these types of schizophrenia see L.P. Thorpe and B. Katz, op. cit., pp. 617-625 and Maslow and Mittelmann, op. cit., pp. 478-498.
8. Moses Buttenwieser, "The Character and Date of Ezekiel's Prophecies," Hebrew Union College Annual, VII, p. 18.
9. Broome, op. cit., p. 278.
10. Ibid., pp. 279-281.
11. Ibid., p. 281.
12. Ibid.
13. Ibid., pp. 282-83.

14. *Ibid.*, p. 291.
15. *Ibid.*, pp. 283-84.
16. *Ibid.*, p. 284.
17. *Ibid.*, pp. 284-85.
18. *Ibid.*, p. 285.
19. *Ibid.*, pp. 285-86.
20. *Ibid.*, p. 287.
21. *Ibid.*, pp. 288-89.
22. *Ibid.*, p. 288.
23. *Ibid.*, p. 290.
24. *Ibid.*, pp. 291-292.
25. Prophetic actions and words were significant partly because they did deviate from the established "norm." In those times there were set patterns of behavior for the prophet of Yahweh and Ezekiel fell into that pattern of speech and activity --with individual variations, of course.
26. Thorpe and Katz, *op. cit.*, p. 622.
27. There is no reason for us to doubt there was a movement toward religious syncretism in Jerusalem during the reign of Zedekiah. Furthermore such a religious trend would necessarily be led by a few leading individuals. Pelatiah and Jaazaniah are pointed out as being just such evil leaders. The fact that Pelatiah is not mentioned outside Ezekiel's book does not prove anything about his existence.
28. Cameron, *op. cit.*, p. 28.
29. The prophet's interpretation of history is clear and extremely accurate on several occasions (cf. chapters 16 and 23). It is hardly admissible that a schizophrenic would be able to interpret historical events and trends in such a remarkable way. He was extremely well informed about the surrounding nations, their past and current history. Chapter 18 is the outcome of a very logical process of thought in a given historical context which would lead to the necessity for an individualistic approach to sin and salvation. This man whose speeches were as a "love-song of one that has a pleasing voice" (33:32b) to his hearers subsequent to Jerusalem's destruction could hardly have been a schizophrenic. His messages change as the real situation is altered and such a general shift of emphasis would be impossible in one who was unable to return completely from his world of phantasy.
30. Herbert W. Hines, "The Prophet as Mystic", AJSL, XL, pp. 37-71.
31. Buttenwieser, *op. cit.*, pp. 1-19; George Widengren, <u>Literary and Psychological Aspects of the Hebrew Prophets</u>, Upsala, 1948, pp. 94-120.
32. Hines, *op. cit.*, p. 51.
33. Broome, *op. cit.*, pp. 280-81.
34. Buttenwieser, *op. cit.*, pp. 7-11.

35. Hines, op. cit., pp. 43, 52-53.
36. Ibid., pp. 43-44.
37. Ibid., p. 44.
38. Ibid., p. 45.
39. "Prophets and mystics are psychologically related; their experiences are similar and seem to contain the same elements. Both have visions of God and hear His voice, both have absolute confidence in Him as their directing activity, and both have the conviction of knowledge conferred in the experience of divine illumination. Briefly, then short periods of rapture, ineffable experiences, seeing or hearing God and learning from Him —these are common to both prophet and mystic," Hines, op. cit., p. 41. For a discussion of the reasons for not identifying the prophetic experience with unio mystica see ZAW, 1940, pp. 65-74 and Albright, Stone Age to Christianity, p. 333.
40. Beryl D. Cohon, The Prophets, New York, 1939, pp. 151-52.
41. We know of not a single case where the subconscious experience of an individual is not couched in terms of conscious background and environment. Ezekiel saw a temple; he had a vision of Yahweh, and he recorded these visions in the terminology of his religious milieu. Teresa saw Christ and the Virgin, El Ghazzali had a vision in Moslem terms and so on. In other words, the mystic clarifies conscious experience and interprets it through unconscious mystical visions.
42. Widengren, op. cit., pp. 118-19.
43. We hold that Ezekiel was taking the broad view of the religious situation as it existed and developed in Jerusalem. The incidents which are depicted in chapter 8 probably never occurred but similar things were happening day by day in' the Holy City. By constantly thinking of these events and trends the prophetic mind would naturally crystallize them into specific visions in which men like Jaazaniah and Pelatiah would most surely appear. For a discussion of the religious syncretism described in chapter 8 see W.F. Albright, Archeology and the Religion of Israel, Baltimore, 1946, pp. 165-68.
44. Buttenwieser, op. cit., p. 17.
45. Widengren and Kittel insist on the power of clairvoyance for Ezekiel. For their discussions see Rudolph Kittel, Geschichte des Volkes Israel, III, pp. 151-58 and G. Widengren, op. cit., p. 111.
46. Hines, op. cit., p. 71.
47. Ibid., pp. 69-71.
48. Kittel, op. cit., p. 164.
49. Ibid., pp. 164ff.
50. W.F. Albright, Stone Age to Christianity, pp. 248-49.

Chapter V

1. Cf. R. Kraetzschmar, Ezechiel, HKAT.

2. Cf. J. Herrmann, *Ezechiel*, Kommentar zum Alten Testament, pp. xvii-xxxiv.
3. G. Hölscher, op. cit.
4. See especially our discussion on dates in Chapter II for an analysis of Torrey's and Smith's views.
5. W.A. Irwin, op. cit., p. 34.
6. *Ibid*.
7. *Ibid*., pp. 33ff.
8. *Ibid*., pp. 269-283.
9. Buttenwieser, op. cit., pp. 16-18.
10. It is our opinion that Herrmann was on the right track in feeling that Ezekiel had some part in the final development of his book. Yet Herrmann is wrong in taking the prophet to be the editor, since linguistic and other evidence almost certainly rule out such a possibility.
11. W. Kessler, *Die innere Einheitlichkeit des Buches Ezechiel*, Herrnhut, 1926.
12. It is important to remember that much which was poetic in the original oracles would most assuredly have been reduced to prose at the time the written record was made. Among other ancient people, poets or prophets in chanting or reciting to music were able to maintain a poetic beat, but once the material was reduced to writing the poetic form often disappeared. Still it may be that the prophet remembered only content, not the form, when his oracles were reduced to writing.

Besides this possibility, it is true that the prophets seem to have tended more to the poetic and the priests to the prosaic. Ezekiel's priestly background would thus be an important factor in the extent of prose found in his prophecy. These are but suggestions which may or may not help to clear up the extent and relation of prose and poetry in the book.
13. It is our thought that Ezekiel often used material which was the common possession of all the people and by interpretation breathed new life and meaning into it. We know that this was done with proverbs and popular stories, hence we would expect the same prophetic technique with respect to older verse.
14. The marvelous descriptions of Tyre and Egypt in all their splendor might have come more logically from one who had seen these wonders and described them in verse than from Ezekiel. The poems were widely known perhaps as nothing more than descriptions, but Ezekiel used the words of others, refashioning them into oracles of destruction.
15. Irwin, op. cit., p. 288f.
16. *Ibid*., pp. 34ff.
17. Much of the genius of Ezekiel, as we understand it, is his ability to reinterpret history (Ez.20), stories (Ez.16 and 23), proverbs (12:21-28) and perhaps poetry (cf. chapters 17, 19, 27, etc.). Irwin's idea that "the false commentary" could

not have come from the prophet is a mistake since logically consistent metaphors were never a necessary part of a prophetic oracle. Indeed, as we have stated, the bad vinewood because of its uselessness must necessarily be destroyed. The same hard logic is applied to the people of the land, who are compared to vinewood.

18. Irwin, op. cit., pp. 289-303.
19. Like many other writers Irwin seems anxious to restore Ezekiel to "prophetic normality," free from all priestly incumbrances and visionary flights.
20. For a discussion of the possible meanings of these names see W.F. Albright, "Contributions to Biblical Archeology and Philology," JBL, XLIII, 1924, pp. 378-385.
21. See Chapter III above.
22. Since our prophet was "overwhelmed" by his first experience of visionary activity, it may well follow that a period of stupor or silence would come upon him after each vision. But when Yahweh spoke, his mouth was opened (3:27).
23. Cf. W.F. Albright, JBL, LI, 1932, p. 96.
24. Spiegel, op. cit.
25. Other similar superscriptions are Joel 1:1, Am. 1:1, Mic. 1:1, Nah. 1:1, Hab. 1:1, Zeph. 1:1, Hag. 1:1 and Zech. 1:1. They are not all as complete as the ones introducing the books of Isaiah and Jeremiah, but their presence at the beginning of so many prophetic books indicates that we should expect such an introductory statement at the head of Ezekiel's prophecy.
26. W.F. Albright, JBL, LI, 1932, p. 97.
27. Although evidence strongly points to the deletion of היה, it is not a necessary part of the emendation. In the case of היה השנה the text is awkward and בשנה seems to be more normal. The error could possibly have arisen when a copyist attempted to transpose yearly and monthly dates.
28. W.F. Albright, op. cit.
29. Herntrich says of the theme: "Wie das Thema einer Bachschen Fuge redet dieser Wille durch das ganze Buch Ezechiel: So sollt ihr erkennen, das ich Jahve bin." Cf. Herntrich, op. cit. p. 130.
30. Cf. Kraetzschmar, op. cit.
31. This very important point has been dealt with in some detail in Chapters II and IV.
32. Our assumption that chapters 40 through 48 circulated for some years, either orally or in manuscript form, is based mainly on the importance of this detailed vision for the Restoration. Since it was of such significance for the future, it must have been written down soon after the twenty-fifth year (40:1).
33. Not only do we have a parallel in the relationship of Jeremiah and Baruch, but linguistic data and literary structure force us to posit some such scribe or group of scribes as

disciples of Ezekiel.

34. We mean by chronological-topical order that a section began with a dated event about a specific subject and then kindred material was drawn to the section without regard to date.

35. "The twenty-seventh year" is further testimony in support of a later publication of the book, most probably in the thirtieth year. It is difficult to explain this date in any other way.

36. The general meaning of these chapters is quite clear, but specific understanding is still beyond our grasp.

www.ingramcontent.com/pod-product-compliance
Lightning Source LLC
Chambersburg PA
CBHW020913090426
42736CB00008B/616